Myths
and
Legends
of the
World

Volume 4

John M. Wickersham
Editor in Chief

Macmillan Reference USA/An Imprint of The Gale Group
New York

Developed for Macmillan Reference USA by
Visual Education Corporation, Princeton, NJ.

For Macmillan

Publisher: Elly Dickason

Editor in Chief: Hélène G. Potter

Cover Design: Irina Lubenskaya

For Visual Education

Project Director: Darryl Kestler

Writers: John Haley, Charles Roebuck, Rebecca Stefoff

Editors: Cindy George, Eleanor Hero, Linda Perrin, Charles Roebuck

Copyediting Supervisor: Helen A. Castro

Indexer: Sallie Steele

Production Supervisor: Marcel Chouteau

Photo Research: Susan Buschhorn, Sara Matthews

Interior Design: Maxson Crandall

Electronic Preparation: Fiona Torphy

Electronic Production: Rob Ehlers, Lisa Evans-Skopas, Laura Millan, Isabelle Ulsh

Macmillan Reference USA
1633 Broadway
New York, NY 10019

Printed in the United States of America
1 2 3 4 5 6 7 8 9 10

Library of Congress Cataloging-in-Publication Data

Myths and legends of the world / John M. Wickersham, editor in chief.
    p. cm.
    Includes bibliographical references and index.
    Contents: v. 1. Abel–Coriolanus — v. 2. Corn–Io — v. 3. Iphigenia–Quetzalcoatl — v. 4. Ra–Zoroastrian mythology.
    ISBN 0-02-865439-0 (set : alk. paper)
    1. Mythology—Juvenile literature. 2. Legends. [1. Mythology—Encyclopedias. 2. Folklore—Encyclopedias.] I. Wickersham, John M. (John Moore), 1943-
BL311 .M97   2000
398.2—dc21   00-030528

Ra (Re)

deity god or goddess
pantheon all the gods of a particular culture
primeval from the earliest times

underworld land of the dead

One of the most important **deities** in Egyptian mythology, the sun god Ra (or Re) was the supreme power in the universe. The giver of life, he was often merged with the god Amun as Amun-Ra. Some myths present Ra as the head of the Egyptian **pantheon** and ruler of all the gods. Others say that he was the only god and that all other deities were merely aspects of Ra.

In some creation myths, Ra emerged from either a **primeval** mound or primeval waters as Ra-Atum and created Tefnut (Moisture) and Shu (Air). From this first divine pair sprang the sky goddess Nut and earth god Geb, who created the universe and gave birth to the gods Osiris†, Isis†, Set†, Nephthys, and Horus.

Ra appeared in many myths and legends, and stories about him varied. As the sun god, he rode across the sky in a golden ship, bringing light and warmth to all creatures living on earth. When the sun set in the evening, he descended to the **underworld** and brought light and air to the people who dwelled there. Each evening Ra's servants helped him battle his eternal enemy, the mighty snake Apep (known also as Apophis), who tried to swallow

The Egyptian sun god Ra traveled across the sky during the day and through the underworld at night. This tomb painting of the 1200s B.C. shows Ra with a sun disk on his head.

cult group bound together by devotion to a particular person, belief, or god

trickster mischievous figure appearing in various forms in the folktales and mythology of many different peoples

Ra and all his creations. Some stories said that Ra sailed along the body of Nut, the sky goddess, during the day and then traveled through her body at night.

According to one series of myths, Ra first ruled during a golden age. Everything he saw was perfect, and the sight of such wonders brought tears to his eyes. The tears fell to earth and grew into human beings. In time, however, Ra became angry with the humans because of their actions. He summoned his divine eye, the beautiful goddess Hathor, and transformed her into Sekhmet, a savage lioness. Ra sent the lioness to earth to kill humans, but after she had caused massive bloodshed, he decided to save the humans that remained. He played a trick on Sekhmet, getting her so drunk on beer that she forgot to continue killing. Nevertheless, death had now been introduced into the world.

In another myth, the goddess Isis wished to learn the secret name of Ra. The name contained great power, which Isis planned to use to make her magical spells stronger. By this time, Ra had become quite old. Isis collected some of the spit that drooled down his chin, mixed it with clay, and made a poisonous snake. One day as Ra was out walking, the snake bit him. Tormented by terrible pain, Ra summoned the other gods to help him. Isis promised to relieve his suffering, but only if he revealed his powerful secret name. He finally agreed, and Isis used the name in a magical spell to remove the poison and heal the sun god.

The chief center for Ra's **cult** in ancient Egypt was the city of Heliopolis (city of the sun). As worship of Ra grew, it challenged the supremacy of all other cults and eventually became a part of them. Ra remained the principal god throughout the history of ancient Egypt, and Egyptian kings claimed to be the sons of Ra in order to link themselves to him. In ancient art, the god is commonly shown with the head of a falcon wearing a shining solar disk on its head. ***See also*** AMUN; ATUM; CREATION STORIES; EGYPTIAN MYTHOLOGY; HATHOR; ISIS; NUT; OSIRIS; SET; SUN; THOTH; UNDERWORLD.

Ragnarok

According to Norse† mythology, the world will end at Ragnarok, a time of great destruction when the gods will wage a final battle with the giants and other evil forces. Ragnarok has not yet arrived, but the events leading to it have already been set in motion.

Before Ragnarok begins, the world will suffer a terrible winter lasting three years. During this period the sun will grow dim, evil forces will be released, and wars will rage among humans. The **trickster** Loki will gather the frost giants and sail to Asgard, the home of gods. The wolf Fenrir, the serpent Jormungand, and Hel, the goddess of the dead, will break free and join Loki and other evil characters in a battle against the gods.

On the morning of Ragnarok, the god Heimdall will sound his mighty horn, summoning the gods to battle. During the terrible struggle that follows, all the great gods—including Odin† and

Thor†—will be killed. Loki and the monsters, giants, and other evil beings will also perish. The earth will be set on fire, the sun and moon will be destroyed, the sky will fall, and the world will finally sink beneath the sea and vanish.

Ragnarok will not be the end of everything, however. The World Tree Yggdrasill will survive, and two humans—Lif and Lifthrasir—and some animals will be sheltered among its branches. New land will rise from the oceans, and a fresh green earth will emerge. Lif and Lifthrasir will repopulate the world. Some of the gods—including Balder†—will also return and rebuild Asgard, ushering in a new golden age. Giants and other evil beings will not reappear but will fade as a distant memory. *See also* **FENRIR; GIANTS; HEIMDALL; HEL; LOKI; MONSTERS; NORSE MYTHOLOGY; ODIN; SERPENTS AND SNAKES; THOR; YGGDRASILL.**

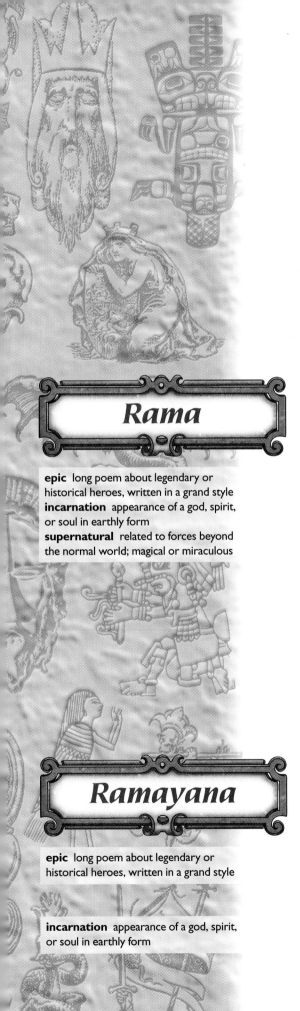

Rama

epic long poem about legendary or historical heroes, written in a grand style
incarnation appearance of a god, spirit, or soul in earthly form
supernatural related to forces beyond the normal world; magical or miraculous

Rama, or Ramachandra, is the hero and main character of the *Ramayana,* one of the most famous **epics** in Hindu literature. The story of Rama's life and adventures figures prominently in this text. As the seventh **incarnation** of the god Vishnu†, Rama inherited part of Vishnu's **supernatural** power. The son of King Dasaratha of Ayodhya and his wife Kausalya, Rama was chosen by the gods to kill the evil demon Ravana.

Rama married Sita, whom Hindu people consider to be the perfect wife. Rama and his brother Lakshmana defeated an army of Rakshasas, a race of evil demons. One of these demons, Ravana, kidnapped Sita and took her to his kingdom in Sri Lanka. With the help of the monkey god Hanuman, Rama and Lakshmana defeated the Rakshasas and killed Ravana.

Rama and Sita were reunited and returned to Ayodhya, where Rama took the throne and ruled for many years. Toward the end of his reign, Sita disappeared into a crack in the earth. In despair at the loss of his wife, Rama walked into the river Sarayu and ended his life. The god Brahma† welcomed him to heaven. *See also* **HINDUISM AND MYTHOLOGY; RAMAYANA; VISHNU.**

Ramayana

epic long poem about legendary or historical heroes, written in a grand style

incarnation appearance of a god, spirit, or soul in earthly form

One of the most famous **epics** in Hindu literature, the *Ramayana* tells of the life and adventures of Rama, a legendary hero who is worshiped as a god in many parts of India. Probably written in the 200s B.C., the *Ramayana* is attributed to Valmiki, a wise man who appears as a character in the work. Based on numerous legends, the *Ramayana* also incorporates sacred material from the Vedas, a series of ancient Hindu religious texts.

Early Life of Rama. According to the *Ramayana,* Rama was the seventh **incarnation** of the god Vishnu†. Born as the eldest son of King Dasaratha of Ayodhya, he was conceived when Vishnu gave three of the king's wives a special potion to drink. Dasaratha's

The *Ramayana*, a famous Hindu epic, tells of the life and adventures of a legendary hero called Rama. This painting from the 1700s illustrates the marriage of Rama and his brothers.

supernatural related to forces beyond the normal world; magical or miraculous

senior wife, Kausalya, gave birth to Rama. The other wives gave birth to Rama's brothers—Bharata and the twins Lakshmana and Satrughna. Rama inherited half of Vishnu's **supernatural** power, while his brothers shared the rest.

The four brothers grew up as close friends, particularly Rama and Lakshmana. One day a wise man named Vishvamitra asked Rama and his brothers to help defeat Taraka, queen of a race of demons called the Rakshasas. Rama and Lakshmana agreed to help, and Rama killed Taraka. Vishvamitra then took the brothers to the court of King Janaka, where Rama entered a contest for the hand of Sita, the king's daughter. By bending and breaking a sacred bow given to the king by the god Shiva, Rama won the contest.

Soon after the marriage of Rama and Sita, King Dasaratha decided to turn over his throne to Rama. However, his wife Kaikeyi, the mother of Bharata, reminded Dasaratha that he had once promised to grant her two wishes. Reluctantly, the king granted Kaikeyi her wishes—to banish Rama and place Bharata on the throne.

A dutiful son, Rama accepted his banishment and went to the Dandaka Forest with Sita and Lakshmana. King Dasaratha died of grief soon after they departed. Bharata had been away during these earlier events. When called back to take the throne, he agreed to rule only during his brother's absence and acknowledged Rama as the rightful king.

Battling the Rakshasas. During their exile in the forest, Rama helped defend the wise men living there against the evil Rakshasas. One of these demons, the hideous giantess Surpanakha, offered to marry both Rama and Lakshmana. When they

† See **Names and Places** at the end of this volume for further information.

refused, the giantess attacked Sita, but the brothers cut off Surpanakha's ears and nose and drove her away. Surpanakha sent her younger brother Khara and an army of demons to avenge her, but Rama and Lakshmana defeated and killed them all.

Furious at this defeat, Surpanakha went to her older brother Ravana, the demon king of Sri Lanka, and plotted revenge. When the giantess told Ravana about the beautiful Sita, he went to Dandaka Forest. Disguised as a beggar, the demon king kidnapped Sita and carried her back to his kingdom. He then tried to get Sita to marry him, but she rejected all his advances—even when he threatened to kill and eat her.

Meanwhile, Rama and Lakshmana set off in search of Sita. Along the way they met the monkey king Sugriva, son of the god Indra, and formed an alliance. They helped him win back his throne from his wicked half brother Bali. In return, the brothers received help from the monkey armies. After the monkey god Hanuman discovered where Sita had been taken, the monkey armies marched to Sri Lanka and defeated the Rakshasas in a series of battles. During the fighting, Rama killed Ravana and was reunited with Sita.

Rama and Sita. After their reunion, Rama wondered whether Sita had remained faithful while held captive by Ravana. Sita proclaimed her innocence and proved it by passing through a fire unharmed. The fire god Agni also spoke on her behalf, and Rama accepted her innocence.

The couple returned to Ayodhya, and Rama began a long reign of peace and prosperity. But the people still questioned Sita's faithfulness. In time, Rama began to doubt her innocence as well, and he banished her. While in exile, Sita found refuge with an old wise man named Valmiki, and she gave birth to Rama's twin sons, Kusa and Lava.

After many years, the two boys visited Ayodhya. When Rama saw them, he recognized them as his sons and called Sita back from exile. Sita returned and protested her innocence again. She called on Mother Earth to verify that she was telling the truth. In response, the earth opened a crack beneath Sita and swallowed her.

Grief stricken by the loss of Sita, Rama asked the gods to end his sorrow. The gods told Rama that he must either enter heaven or stay on earth. Rama chose to follow Sita to eternity, so he walked into the river Sarayu and drowned. Upon Rama's death, the god Brahma† welcomed the hero into heaven. ***See also*** BRAHMA; DEVILS AND DEMONS; HINDUISM AND MYTHOLOGY; INDRA; RAMA; VEDAS; VISHNU.

Rangi and Papa

deity god or goddess

In Polynesian mythology, Rangi (Father Sky) and Papa (Mother Earth) were the two supreme creator **deities**. They were the source from which all things in the universe originated, including other gods, humans, and the various creatures and features of the earth. Rangi and Papa played an especially important role in the mythology of the Maori people of New Zealand.

primal earliest; existing before other things

chaos great disorder or confusion

According to Maori mythology, Rangi and Papa were created from two **primal** beings—Te Po (night) and Te Kore (emptiness)—who existed in a darkness of **chaos** before the creation of the universe. From the beginning, Rangi and Papa were locked together in a tight and continuing embrace. Into the darkness between their bodies sprang many offspring, including numerous gods.

Trapped between the bodies of their parents, the deities had little space to move around and no light to see. Weary of this situation, the offspring discussed how they could escape the confines of their existence. Tu, the god of war, suggested that they kill Rangi and Papa, but Tane, the god of the forests, had a different solution. Tane suggested that they make space for themselves by separating their parents. The other gods agreed with this plan except for the wind god Tawhiri, who roared his disapproval.

Several of the gods attempted to separate Rangi and Papa. The first to try was Rongo, the god of cultivated plants. Although he pushed with all his might, he was unable to separate the couple. Next to try was Tangaroa, the god of the sea. He also failed, as did Haumia, the god of wild plants and vegetables, and Tu, the war god. Finally, it was time for Tane to try. The god of the forests placed his head on his mother Papa, raised his feet in the air, and pushed upward against his father Rangi. Using all his might, Tane finally separated Rangi and Papa, pushing Rangi up into the sky and pressing Papa to the earth.

With Rangi and Papa separated, the space between them became flooded with light. The various deities, humans, and other offspring who had been trapped there scattered into the world. Freed at last, the children of Rangi and Papa began to quarrel among themselves, especially Tane and the sea god Tangaroa. Polynesians believe that the conflicts between the gods cause such things as the growth of weeds in fields, the differences between humans and animals, and the storms that threaten boats at sea.

Heartbroken at being separated from his beloved Papa, Rangi cried. His tears rained down upon the earth from the sky, causing great flooding. At the same time, the wind god Tawhiri showed his anger with his brothers by sending storms and winds to batter the earth, causing great destruction to the forests, seas, and fields. Only the war god Tu could resist his brother, but their struggle flooded the earth, leaving only the islands of Polynesia.

Over time the offspring of Rangi and Papa multiplied and filled the earth with life. But Rangi still cries from time to time when he misses Papa, and his tears fall as rain or as drops of morning dew. *See also* CREATION STORIES; POLYNESIAN MYTHOLOGY.

Reincarnation

Many cultures have myths and legends that tell of heroes or other characters who die and then come back to life. When they reappear, though, it is not as their former selves but as other people, as animals, or even as plants. The concept of reincarnation—a reappearance of a spirit or soul in earthly form—is based on the

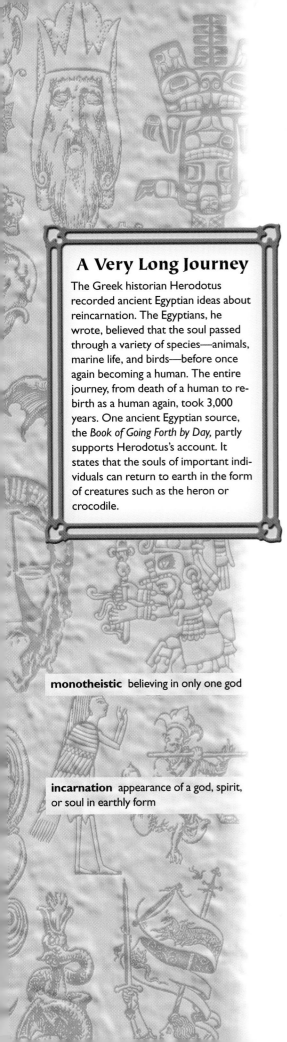

belief that a person's soul continues to exist after death and can transmigrate, or move, to another living thing.

Belief in reincarnation has been shared by a wide variety of peoples, including the ancient Egyptians and Greeks and the Aboriginal people of central Australia. The most complex and influential ideas about reincarnation are found in Asian religions, particularly Hinduism and Buddhism.

Beliefs About Reincarnation. Cultural groups that believe in reincarnation have different ideas about the way it takes place. Some say that human souls come from a general source of life-giving energy. Others claim that particular individuals are repeatedly reborn or come back to life in their descendants.

In Australia, most Aborigines believe that human souls come from spirits left behind by ancestral beings who roamed the earth during a mythical period called Dreamtime. The birth of a child is caused by an ancestral spirit entering a woman's body. The spirit waits in a sacred place for the woman to pass by. After death, the person's spirit returns to the ancestral powers.

According to traditional African belief, the souls or spirits of recently dead people linger near the grave for a time, seeking other bodies—reptile, mammal, bird, or human—to inhabit. Many African traditions link reincarnation to the worship of ancestors, who may be reborn as their own descendants or as animals associated with their clans or groups. The Zulu people of southern Africa believe that a person's soul is reborn many times in the bodies of different animals, ranging in size from tiny insects to large elephants, before being born as a human again. The Yoruba and Edo of western Africa share the widely held notion that people are the reincarnations of their ancestors. They call boys "Father Has Returned" and girls "Mother Has Returned."

Reincarnation plays a central role in Buddhism and Hinduism. It also appears in Jainism and Sikhism, two faiths that grew out of Hinduism and are still practiced in India. Jainism shares with Hinduism a belief in many gods. Sikhism, a **monotheistic** religion, combines some elements of Islam with Hinduism.

Hinduism, Buddhism, Jainism, and Sikhism all began in India, where the idea of rebirth first appears in texts dating from about 700 B.C. They share a belief in samsara—the wheel of birth and rebirth—and karma—the idea that an individual's future **incarnation** depends on the way he or she lived. People who have done good deeds and led moral lives are reborn into higher social classes; those who have not are doomed to return as members of the lower classes or as animals. Only by achieving the highest state of spiritual development can a person escape samsara altogether.

Myths and Legends of Reincarnation. Many world myths and legends feature some form of reincarnation. Ancient Norse† kings were regarded as reincarnations of the god Freyr. After the introduction of Christianity to Norway, some people believed

A Very Long Journey

The Greek historian Herodotus recorded ancient Egyptian ideas about reincarnation. The Egyptians, he wrote, believed that the soul passed through a variety of species—animals, marine life, and birds—before once again becoming a human. The entire journey, from death of a human to re-birth as a human again, took 3,000 years. One ancient Egyptian source, the *Book of Going Forth by Day*, partly supports Herodotus's account. It states that the souls of important individuals can return to earth in the form of creatures such as the heron or crocodile.

monotheistic believing in only one god

incarnation appearance of a god, spirit, or soul in earthly form

Reincarnation

pagan term used by early Christians to describe non-Christians and non-Christian beliefs

the Christian king Saint Olaf was the reincarnation of an earlier **pagan** king, also named Olaf.

In the Arctic regions, where animals are critical to survival, the Inuit people believe that animals as well as humans have souls that are reborn. Hunters must perform ceremonies for the creatures they kill so that the animal spirits can be reborn and hunted in the future. When a person dies, part of his or her soul will be incarnated in the next baby born into the community. Giving the newborn the dead person's name ensures that the child will have some of the ancestor's qualities.

Buddhist tradition includes a set of tales called the Jatakas that are based on reincarnation. They tell of Gautama Buddha's various lives and how he grew wiser and more holy as his soul transmigrated from life to life. In one incarnation Buddha was a hare who sought spiritual growth through fasting. He realized that if a beggar appeared he would have no food to offer, so he decided that he would offer his own flesh. One of the gods came down from heaven and visited the hare in the form of a beggar. The hare willingly hurled himself into a fire to provide a meal for his guest, but the god then saved the hare and painted his image on the moon to honor his spirit of self-sacrifice. On his way to becoming Buddha, Gautama passed through more than 500 lives that included incarnations as an elephant, a priest, a prince, and a hermit.

The Japanese legend of O-Tei illustrates the haunting appeal of the idea of reincarnation. O-Tei was a young girl engaged to be married. She fell ill, and as she lay dying she promised her future husband that she would come back in a healthier body. She died, and the young man wrote a promise to marry her if she ever returned.

Reincarnation plays a central role in Hinduism. People who have performed good deeds and led moral lives are reborn into higher social classes; those who have failed in these areas are doomed to return as members of the lower classes or as animals. This carving of two men with a wheel represents the cycle of birth and rebirth.

Time passed, and eventually he married another woman and had a child. But his wife and child also died. Hoping to heal his grief, the man went on a journey. In a village he had never visited, he stayed in an inn where a girl who looked much like O-Tei waited on him. He asked her name and, speaking in the voice of his first love, she told him that it was O-Tei. She said that she knew of his promise and had returned to him. Then she fainted. When the girl awoke, she had no memory of her former life or what she had said to the man. The two were married and lived happily together. ***See also* AFTER-LIFE; AUSTRALIAN MYTHOLOGY; BUDDHISM AND MYTHOLOGY; HINDUISM AND MYTHOLOGY.**

Rhea

See *Cybele.*

Rig-Veda

One of the earliest and most important religious texts of ancient India, the *Rig-Veda* is the oldest of the four collections of hymns and other sacred texts known as the Vedas. These works are considered the "sacred knowledge" of the Aryans, a people who invaded India in about 1600 B.C. As the Aryans settled in India, their beliefs developed into the Hindu religion, and the *Rig-Veda* and the other Vedas became the most sacred Hindu texts.

The Vedas were composed between 1500 and 1000 B.C. in Vedic Sanskrit, an ancient Indo-European language. Transmitted orally for hundreds of years, they were eventually written down. By about 300 B.C., the Vedas had taken on their current form.

The *Rig-Veda* contains 1,028 mantras, or hymns, directed to the gods and natural forces. The mantras are organized into ten books called mandalas, or circles. According to ancient Hindu tradition, the mantras were based on divine **revelations** received by members of a particular family. Several families put the mantras together to form the different mandalas. Within each mandala, the mantras are organized according to the **deities** with whom they are associated.

Many of the mantras in the *Rig-Veda* are hymns to the gods, praising them for their help in battle and asking for such benefits as wealth, good health, long life, protection, and victory in battle. Besides hymns of praise, the mantras contain blessings and curses. Originally, the mantras were meant to be chanted as part of religious **rites,** and this was the primary way in which the people communicated with the gods.

The *Rig-Veda* and other Vedas express various Hindu beliefs about such matters as the worship of the gods, marriage and funeral rites, and animal sacrifice. The *Rig-Veda* also contains ideas that served as the basis for India's system of **castes.** The text describes how pieces of the god Purusha developed into different classes of society, from the upper-class Brahmans, or priests, through the merchant and farmer classes, down to the Sudra, who were slaves and servants.

revelation communication of divine truth or divine will

deity god or goddess

rite ceremony or formal procedure

caste division of people in Hindu society into classes based on birth

Considered one of the foundations of the Hindu religion, the *Rig-Veda* is also an important source of mythology about Hindu gods and the Aryan deities that came before them. Among the gods to whom its hymns are directed are the supreme god Indra; the fire god Agni; the sky god Varuna; the sun god Surya; and Rudra, a god associated with mountains and storms who later developed into the god Shiva. The god Vishnu, who plays only a minor role in the *Rig-Veda,* later became one of the most important and popular Hindu deities. ***See also*** BRAHMA; HINDUISM AND MYTHOLOGY; INDRA; SHIVA; UPANISHADS; VARUNA; VEDAS; VISHNU.

Rip van Winkle

Rip van Winkle, the hero of a short story by the American writer Washington Irving, was based on an old German legend. Rip was a cheerful but lazy farmer in upstate New York. Always willing to help others, Rip neglected his own home and chores, causing his wife to nag him constantly. One day Rip went hunting in the Catskill Mountains and met a strange-looking little man carrying a keg of liquor. Rip helped the man carry the barrel to a place in the mountains where he saw many similar people playing a bowling game. Rip drank some of the liquor and fell asleep.

Twenty years later, Rip awoke to find his world completely changed. During his long sleep, his wife and most of his friends had died, and the American Revolution had taken place. At first, no one believed his story, but a young woman explained that her father, Rip van Winkle, had gone away 20 years ago. Rip later learned that the little men he saw were the ghosts of Henry Hudson's crew who had discovered the Hudson River.

Robin Hood

Robin Hood was the legendary bandit of England who stole from the rich to help the poor. The stories about Robin appealed to common folk because he stood up against—and frequently outwitted—people in power. Furthermore, his life in the forest—hunting and feasting with his fellow outlaws, coming to the assistance of those in need—seemed like a great and noble adventure.

Early Sources. The earliest known mention of Robin Hood is in William Langland's 1377 work called *Piers Plowman,* in which a character mentions that he knows "rimes of Robin Hood." This and other references from the late 1300s suggest that Robin Hood was well established as a popular legend by that time.

One source of that legend may lie in the old French custom of celebrating May Day. A character called Robin des Bois, or Robin of the Woods, was associated with this spring festival and may have been transplanted to England—with a slight name change. May Day celebrations in England in the 1400s featured a festival "king" called Robin Hood.

A collection of **ballads** about the outlaw Robin Hood, *A Lytell Geste of Robin Hode,* was published in England around 1489. From it and other **medieval** sources, scholars know that Robin

ballad popular song, often telling a story
medieval relating to the Middle Ages in Europe, a period from about A.D. 500 to 1500

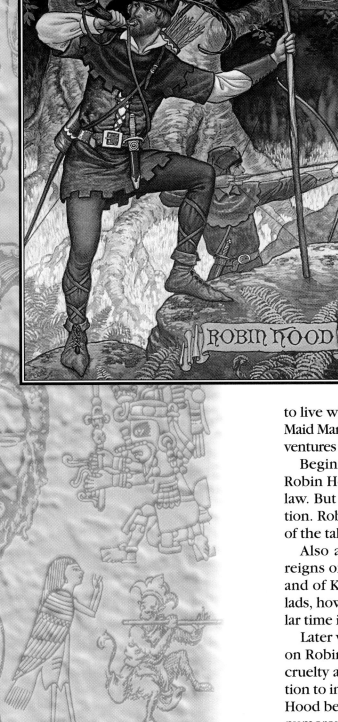

ROBIN HOOD

Robin Hood, the legendary thief of England, stole from the rich and gave the wealth to the poor. Stories about his life and adventures first appeared in the late 1400s.

was originally associated with several locations in England. One was Barnsdale, in the northern district called Yorkshire. The other was Sherwood Forest in Nottinghamshire, where his principal opponent was the vicious and oppressive Sheriff of Nottingham. Robin's companions included Little John, Alan-a-Dale, Much, and Will Scarlett.

The Robin Hood ballads reflect the discontent of ordinary people with political conditions in medieval England. They were especially upset about new laws that kept them from hunting freely in forests that were now claimed as the property of kings and nobles. Social unrest and rebellion swirled through England at the time the Robin Hood ballads first became popular. This unrest erupted in an event called the Peasants' Revolt of 1381.

Later Versions. By the 1500s, more elaborate versions of the legend had begun to appear. Some of these suggested that Robin was a nobleman who had fallen into disgrace and had taken to the woods to live with other outlaws. Robin also acquired a girlfriend named Maid Marian and a new companion, a monk called Friar Tuck. His adventures were then definitely linked to Sherwood Forest.

Beginning in the 1700s, various scholars attempted to link Robin Hood with a real-life figure—either a nobleman or an outlaw. But none of their theories have stood up to close examination. Robin was most likely an imaginary creation, although some of the tales may have been associated with a real outlaw.

Also at about this time, Robin began to be linked with the reigns of King Richard I, "The Lionhearted," who died in 1189, and of King John, who died in 1216. The original medieval ballads, however, contain no references to these kings or to a particular time in which Robin was supposed to have lived.

Later versions of the Robin Hood legend placed more emphasis on Robin's nobility and on his romance with Marian than on the cruelty and social tension that appear in the early ballads. In addition to inspiring many books and poems over the centuries, Robin Hood became the subject of several operas and, in modern times, numerous movies.

Tales of Robin Hood. One of the medieval ballads about Robin Hood involved Sir Guy of Gisborne. Robin and his comrade Little John had an argument and parted. While Little John was on his own, the Sheriff of Nottingham captured him and tied him to a tree. Robin ran into Sir Guy, who had sworn to slay the outlaw

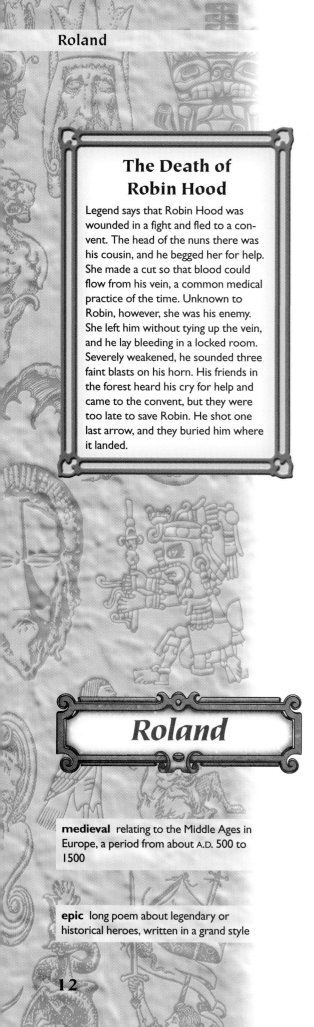

The Death of Robin Hood

Legend says that Robin Hood was wounded in a fight and fled to a convent. The head of the nuns there was his cousin, and he begged her for help. She made a cut so that blood could flow from his vein, a common medical practice of the time. Unknown to Robin, however, she was his enemy. She left him without tying up the vein, and he lay bleeding in a locked room. Severely weakened, he sounded three faint blasts on his horn. His friends in the forest heard his cry for help and came to the convent, but they were too late to save Robin. He shot one last arrow, and they buried him where it landed.

Roland

medieval relating to the Middle Ages in Europe, a period from about A.D. 500 to 1500

epic long poem about legendary or historical heroes, written in a grand style

leader. When they each discovered the other's identity, they drew their swords and fought. Robin killed Sir Guy and put on his clothes.

Disguised as Sir Guy, Robin persuaded the sheriff to let him kill Little John, who was still tied to the tree. However, instead of slaying Little John, Robin freed him, and the two outlaws drove off the sheriff's men.

Another old story, known as Robin Hood and the Monk, also began with a quarrel between Robin and John. Robin went into Nottingham to attend church, but a monk recognized him and raised the alarm. Robin killed 12 people before he was captured.

When word of his capture reached Robin's comrades in the forest, they planned a rescue. As the monk passed by on his way to tell the king of Robin's capture, Little John and Much seized and beheaded him. John and Much, in disguise, visited the king in London and then returned to Nottingham bearing documents sealed with the royal seal. The sheriff, not recognizing them, welcomed the two men and treated them to a feast. That night Little John and Much killed Robin's jailer and set Robin free. By the time the sheriff realized what had happened, the three outlaws were safe in Sherwood Forest.

Robin Hood's role as the enemy of the people who held power and the protector of the poor was clearly illustrated in lines from *A Lytell Geste of Robin Hode.* Robin instructed his followers to do no harm to farmers or countrymen, but to "beat and bind" the bishops and archbishops and never to forget the chief villain, the high sheriff of Nottingham. Some ballads ended with the sheriff's death; in others, the outlaws merely embarrassed the sheriff and stole his riches. In one ballad, the sheriff was robbed and then forced to dress in outlaw green and dine with Robin and his comrades in the forest.

Over time, the image of Robin as a clever, lighthearted prankster gained strength. The tales in which he appeared as a highway robber and murderer were forgotten or rewritten.

Roland was the bravest and most loyal of the 12 legendary paladins, or knights, who served Charlemagne, king of the Franks†. Although Charlemagne was a historical figure, many fanciful tales about the king and his knights appeared during the Middle Ages. It was said that Roland stood 8 feet tall and carried a magical sword called Durindana (or Durendal) that had once belonged to the Trojan hero Hector.

According to **medieval** stories, Roland (or Orlando) was the son of Charlemagne's sister. Living as a poor peasant in Italy, he was welcomed to the court of the king after his true identity was revealed. Although a powerful warrior, Roland's concern with winning honor and fame eventually cost him his life.

The story of Roland's death is told in the famous **epic** the *Song of Roland.* The poem concerns Charlemagne's defeat by the Muslims in Spain in 778. Charlemagne had sent a paladin named

† *See **Names and Places** at the end of this volume for further information.*

Ganelon to negotiate with the Muslim leader. Instead, jealous of Roland, Ganelon plotted with the enemy and revealed the route Roland's army planned to take. The Muslims waited for Roland and ambushed him at Roncesvalles in the Pyrenees Mountains.

The paladins had told Roland to blow his ivory horn to summon reinforcements from Charlemagne, but Roland refused to call for help until the battle was almost lost. By then it was too late. When Charlemagne's troops arrived, Roland and many of the bravest paladins were dead. At the end of the story, Charlemagne had Ganelon killed for his treachery. *See also* **CHARLEMAGNE; HEROES; PALADINS.**

Roman Mythology

pantheon all the gods of a particular culture

deity god or goddess

From the founding of the Roman empire to its fall in A.D. 476, Rome dominated Europe and much of North Africa, the Near East, and Asia Minor†. Although this sprawling empire encompassed many cultures with their own myths and legends, the mythology of the Romans themselves revolved around the founding, history, and heroes of the city of Rome. The Romans had developed their own **pantheon** of gods and goddesses. After they conquered Greece, however, their **deities** became increasingly associated with the figures of Greek mythology.

Background and Sources. Although Rome's early history is difficult to separate from the legends that formed around it, the city appears to have begun as a community of central Italian peoples known as Latins. The Latins merged with the Etruscans, who had come to Italy from Asia Minor before 800 B.C.

Until 510 B.C., Rome was ruled by kings. Then it became a republic governed by elected officials. The Roman republic eventually dominated most of Italy and conquered the North African coast and Greece. By 31 B.C., Rome governed all the lands around the Mediterranean Sea as well as northwest Europe.

The principal sources of information about Roman mythology appeared during the early years of the empire, between about 20 B.C. and A.D. 20. The poet Virgil produced Rome's national **epic,** the *Aeneid,* which drew on myths that linked the city's founding with Greek deities and legends. Another poet, Ovid, wrote the *Metamorphoses,* a collection of Near Eastern and Greek myths that the Romans had adopted. Ovid's *Fasti* describes Roman myths about the gods according to the festivals in their calendar. In his history of Rome, Livy portrayed legends about the city's founding as though they were historical events. These and other writers worked to create an "official" Roman mythology, one that gave Rome an ancient, distinguished, and glorious heritage.

epic long poem about legendary or historical heroes, written in a grand style

Major Deities. In their early years, Roman people had many gods and goddesses called *numina,* or powers. Unlike the Greek deities, the *numina* did not have distinctive, well-defined personalities and characteristics. Few stories about them existed. They were simply the forces that oversaw the activities of daily

patron special guardian, protector, or supporter

life. Examples include Janus, god of doorways and archways, and Terminus, god of boundaries. Many early Roman deities were **patrons** of farming, crops, or the land. Sylvanus, for example, was the protector of woodcutters and plowmen. Other early deities represented virtues or qualities, such as Concordia (goddess of agreement), Fides (goddess of honesty), and Fortuna (goddess of fate or luck).

Captivated by the elaborate and entertaining myths the Greeks had woven around their gods and goddesses, the Romans gradually changed some of their *numina* into Roman versions of the major Greek deities. The ancient Roman god Saturn, guardian of seeds and planting, became identified with the Titan† Cronus, who appeared in Greek mythology as the ancestor of the gods. Aphrodite became Venus, the Roman goddess of love. Zeus and Hera, the king and queen of the Greek gods, became the Roman Jupiter (sometimes called Jove) and Juno.

Mars, a Roman deity first associated with agriculture, took on the characteristics of Ares, the Greek god of war, which explains why the Roman version of this god is concerned with both war and farming. Diana, a traditional Roman goddess of the forests, was identified with Artemis, the Greek goddess of the hunt. Minerva was the Roman version of Athena†, Neptune of Poseidon†, Vulcan

This fresco from the ancient Roman city of Pompeii shows the courtship of Mars and Venus. Mars, the Roman god of agriculture and war, was identified with Ares, the Greek god of war. Venus, the Roman goddess of love and beauty, was linked to the Greek goddess Aphrodite.

†*See **Names and Places** at the end of this volume for further information.*

of Hephaestus†, Mercury of Hermes†, Ceres of Demeter†, and Bacchus of Dionysus†. Apollo†, too, was brought into the Roman pantheon, where he was known as both Apollo and Phoebus.

The Romans gave their deities some of the characteristics and even some of the stories associated with the Greek gods and goddesses. They also imported other foreign deities, such as Cybele from near Troy in Asia Minor and the Persian god Mithras. At the same time, in their own homes they continued to worship their traditional household gods, known as the Lares and Penates.

Roman mythology also includes human heroes. Sometimes these mortals became deities. Romulus, the legendary founder of the city of Rome, was thought to have become the god Quirinus. Many emperors were declared gods by the Roman senate after their deaths, and people worshiped them in temples. The most honored heroes, however, were Aeneas, Romulus and Remus, and others from myths about Rome's beginnings and early history.

Major Myths and Themes. Romans cherished myths about their city's founding. A myth that probably dates from around 400 B.C. told of the twins Romulus and Remus, offspring of a Latin princess and the god Mars. Although their uncle tried to drown them, they survived under the care of a she-wolf and a woodpecker. Eventually, the twins overthrew their uncle and decided to found a new city on the spot where they had been rescued by the she-wolf. After receiving an **omen** from the gods about the new city, Romulus killed Remus and became leader—as the gods had intended. Rome took its name from him.

The ditch that Romulus dug to mark the boundary of Rome was called the *pomerium.* Everything within the *pomerium* was considered to be part of the original, authentic, sacred Rome. Throughout Rome's long history, the Romans preserved landmarks within the *pomerium* that they associated with the legend of Romulus and Remus. These included a cave on the Palatine Hill where the wolf was said to have nursed the twins and a nearby hut where Romulus was said to have lived.

According to legend, Romulus made the new city a refuge for criminals, poor people, and runaway slaves to attract citizens. Because this population lacked women, Romulus invited a neighboring people called the Sabines to a religious festival and then kidnapped the Sabine women. Titus Tatius, king of the Sabines, brought an army to wage war on Rome. By that time, however, the Sabine women had married Romans. At their urging, the men made peace, and until his death, Titus ruled at the side of Romulus.

One myth connected with the war between the Romans and the Sabines says that a high-ranking Roman woman named Tarpeia caught sight of Tatius and fell in love with him. Tarpeia betrayed Rome to the Sabine army, but Tatius slew her for her treachery. The myth became part of the city's geography—a rocky outcropping from which the Romans cast murderers and traitors to their deaths was called the Tarpeian Hill. Other legendary figures from Rome's early history include the virtuous wife Lucretia and the

Raising the Sun

One of Rome's most worshiped goddesses received little literary attention. According to legend, Angerona knew a magical spell to raise the sun in midwinter. Her festival occurred on December 21, the shortest day of the year, when she was believed to say the words that would cause the days to lengthen and spring to return. Even more important, Angerona guarded the secret name of the city of Rome. The gods knew this name, but Rome would be doomed if people ever learned it. Statues of Angerona showed her mouth covered with her hands or a gag so that the secret name could not slip out.

omen sign of future events

A famous Roman myth tells of the she-wolf that cared for Romulus and Remus in a cave. Romulus later killed Remus and founded the city of Rome on the spot where they had met the she-wolf.

brave soldier Horatius, both of whom appear in tales about the downfall of the monarchy and the founding of the republic.

By the late years of the republic, Romans had adopted a powerful new myth about their state's origins. This account is most fully told in the *Aeneid.* It revolves around Aeneas, a Trojan† prince who fled from his ruined homeland because the gods told him that he was fated to establish a "new Troy." After wandering around the Mediterranean, Aeneas landed in Italy with some Trojan followers. There he married the daughter of the local Latin king; Aeneas's son Ascanius founded a settlement called Alba Longa. This version of Roman history emphasized the idea that the gods had always meant for Rome to rule the world. Romulus and Remus became sons of a princess of Alba Longa, descendants of Aeneas—a perfect example of Roman willingness and ability to piece together different myths.

Myths arose linking many deities with key events in Roman history. The twin wind gods Castor and Pollux, together called the Dioscuri, appear in both Greek and Roman mythology as inseparable brothers who form the constellation Gemini. In the Roman version, the Dioscuri fought on the side of the Roman army in a battle in the 490s B.C., and they brought word of the Roman victory back to the city.

The myths and legends about Roman history celebrate the virtues that Romans especially prized: duty, self-sacrifice, honor, bravery, and **piety.** Roman deities, too, tended to represent virtues, without the all-too-human weaknesses and vices of the Greek gods. A Greek historian named Dionysius of Halicarnassus recognized this difference when he wrote that the Roman deities were more moral than the Greek deities because the Romans had taken only what was good from the old stories and left out all the disgraceful parts.

Legacy. The influence of Roman mythology extended farther and lasted longer than the Roman empire. Statues, temples, and other structures associated with Roman gods and myths can be found far from the ancient capital. An old **mosaic** in Britain, for example, shows the she-wolf feeding Romulus and Remus. It is a reminder of the days when Rome ruled Britain and a mark of how far Roman mythology spread.

The **Renaissance** began with a new interest in ancient Greece and Rome. The mythology of these cultures became part of the store of knowledge of well-educated Europeans. Since that time, hundreds of artists, writers, and musical composers have found

piety faithfulness to beliefs

mosaic picture made up of many small colored stones or tiles

Renaissance artistic and intellectual movement that spread across Europe from the late 1300s through the 1500s

†*See **Names and Places** at the end of this volume for further information.*

inspiration in the *Aeneid* and in Rome's heavily mythologized version of its history. ***See also*** AENEAS; AENEID, THE; APOLLO; CASTOR AND POLLUX; CYBELE; DIANA; GREEK MYTHOLOGY; HORATIUS; JANUS; LARES AND PENATES; LUCRETIA; METAMORPHOSES, THE; MITHRAS; NEPTUNE; OVID; ROMULUS AND REMUS; SATURN; TROJAN WAR; VENUS; VESTA.

Romulus and Remus

Vestal Virgin priestess of the Roman goddess Vesta who was required to remain a virgin

omen sign of future events

In Roman mythology, Romulus and Remus were the twin sons of the god Mars† and the founders of the city of Rome. Their mother, Rhea Silvia, was the only daughter of King Numitor of Alba Longa. Numitor's brother Amulius seized the throne and forced Rhea Silvia to become a **Vestal Virgin.** He wanted to make sure that she had no children who would have a claim to the throne. However, Rhea Silvia was raped by Mars and gave birth to Romulus and Remus.

Early Years. When Amulius found out about the twins, he ordered that they be thrown into the Tiber River to drown. The boys floated downstream, coming ashore near a sacred fig tree. A she-wolf and a woodpecker—creatures sacred to Mars—fed the twins and kept them alive until a shepherd found them. Faustulus, the shepherd, and his wife raised the boys. They grew up to be brave and bold.

The twins became involved in local conflicts and led a group of youths on raids, including a raid on a herd of cattle that belonged to Numitor. Remus was caught and brought before Numitor. In questioning the young man, Numitor realized that Remus was his grandson. Shortly afterward, the twins led a revolt against Amulius. They killed him and put Numitor back on the throne.

Founding of Rome. Romulus and Remus wanted to found a city of their own, so they returned to the place where Faustulus had discovered them. An **omen** determined that Romulus should be the founder of the new city. He marked out the city boundaries and began to build a city wall. When Remus jumped over the unfinished wall, mocking his brother for thinking that it could keep anyone out of the city, Romulus killed him. Romulus became the sole leader of the new city, named Rome.

The Rape of the Sabine Women. To populate Rome, Romulus invited people who had fled from nearby areas to live there. However, most of these settlers were men. The city needed women. Romulus invited the Sabine people, who lived in neighboring towns, to come to Rome for a great festival. While the Sabine men were enjoying themselves, the Romans seized the Sabine maidens, drove the men from the city, and married their women. The event became known as The Rape of the Sabine Women.

The Sabine men planned revenge and staged several small but unsuccessful raids. Then Titus Tatius, the Sabine king, led an army against Rome. The Romans were losing the battle when Romulus prayed to Jupiter† for help. At that point, the Sabine women stepped in. They pleaded with the warring men to stop, for they

Round Table

dowry money, goods, or property that a woman brings to her husband at marriage

Holy Grail sacred cup said to have been used by Jesus Christ at the Last Supper

Sacrifice

deity god or goddess

could not bear to see their fathers and husbands killing one another. The two sides agreed to a peace in which the Sabines and Romans formed a union, with Rome as the capital.

Romulus ruled Rome for 40 years. He disappeared mysteriously while reviewing his army on the Campus Martius (Field of Mars) in a thunderstorm. ***See also*** **ROMAN MYTHOLOGY; TWINS.**

Arthurian legends† tell of a great Round Table in King Arthur's court at Camelot at which the king held meetings with his knights. Usually a king sat at the head of a royal table with his closest companions gathered around him. However, because the Round Table had no head or foot, none of the knights who sat at it could claim a more important position than the others. For this reason, the Round Table was a symbol of the equality that existed in Arthur's court.

According to legend, the magician Merlin created the table for Arthur's father, Uther Pendragon. After Uther died, the table came into the hands of a local king named Leodegran. In time, Leodegran's daughter Guinevere married Arthur, and Leodegran gave the table to Arthur as part of Guinevere's **dowry.**

The Round Table was supposedly patterned after a table made to commemorate the Last Supper of Jesus Christ. One of the seats at that table was left empty to symbolize Judas, the apostle who betrayed Jesus. King Arthur's Round Table also had an empty seat, known as the Siege Perilous. It was said that the only person who could safely occupy the Siege Perilous was the knight who would find the **Holy Grail.** When Sir Galahad came to Camelot, the Siege Perilous became his seat.

The other seats around the table bore the names of the knights who had earned the right to occupy them. When a knight of the Round Table died or left the court, his seat could be taken only by someone who was braver than the previous occupant. If a pretender tried to take a seat at the table, a magic force would throw him out of it. ***See also*** **ARTHUR, KING; ARTHURIAN LEGENDS; CAMELOT; GALAHAD; GUINEVERE; HOLY GRAIL; MERLIN.**

Many religious ceremonies have included sacrifice, the act of giving up something of value and offering it to a **deity.** Worshipers may make a sacrifice to win the favor of the deity, to give thanks, or to maintain a good relationship with the god. Myths from around the world contain many examples of sacrifices in which animals, humans, and even gods shed blood or die. Sometimes the sacrifice is linked with creation or with the continuation of life on earth. People also make offerings of precious items such as flowers, wine, and incense or a portion of the fruit or grain collected during a harvest.

Meaning and Methods of Sacrifice. One type of sacrifice involves the offering of blood or life. According to one theory, the

One type of sacrifice, which was practiced by the Aztecs of Mexico, involved blood offerings to feed the gods. Aztec priests conducted elaborate ceremonies of human sacrifice.

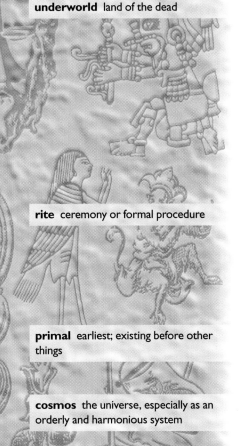

underworld land of the dead

rite ceremony or formal procedure

primal earliest; existing before other things

cosmos the universe, especially as an orderly and harmonious system

practice of blood sacrifice was based on the belief that life is precious, even divine. When freed from an earthly body, life returned to its sacred source. In ancient Rome, a person performing a sacrifice said to the god, "Be thou increased by this offering." The idea behind this type of sacrifice was not pain, suffering, or death. Rather, life was being returned to the divine world so that the gods, in turn, would continue to give life to the human world.

Other theories provide different explanations for blood sacrifice. One suggests that it began as a form of magic. Another says that sacrifice may have been viewed as a symbolic meal that the community shared with its deity or as a reenactment of creation myths. Still another tells that sacrifice may have been seen as a way of focusing and controlling aggression within the community.

Hunting peoples generally sacrificed game animals, while herding and farming peoples used domestic animals such as sheep, goats, chickens, and cattle. Certain types of animals were regarded as the most appropriate sacrifices for particular purposes or for particular deities. Dark-colored animals, for example, might be offered to deities of the **underworld,** while an all-white animal might be seen as the best gift for a sky god.

The sacrifice of humans has been known in many parts of the world. There is also evidence that in some communities animals were eventually substituted for human victims. The method of slaughter generally involved either blood (flowing freely or offered in a ceremonial vessel), fire (to carry the sacrifice to the god), or both. Sometimes, however, the person to be sacrificed was strangled, hanged, or drowned.

A special person, such as a ruler, priest, head of household, or older member of the community, usually supervised or carried out the sacrifice. The sacrifice was made in front of a group—it was too important an act to be performed privately. Special **rites,** such as ceremonial bathing or fasting, often accompanied the sacrifice. The sacrificial offering might be placed on an altar or before a statue of a deity or burned in a sacred fire so that the smoke would carry its scent to the heavens.

Mythic Sacrifices. Many creation myths involve self-sacrifice by gods or **primal** beings. In an early Hindu myth, Purusha is the primal being who allows himself to be dismembered so that creation can take place. His eye becomes the sun, his head the sky, his breath the wind, and so on. Purusha became a symbol of the acts of sacrifice that kept the **cosmos** stable. The mythology of the Aztecs of central Mexico told how two of the gods formed the

19

prophecy foretelling of what is to come; also something that is predicted

universe by splitting a goddess in half, so that one part of her became the sky and the other part became the earth. The Aztecs performed large-scale, violent rites of human sacrifice as a way of repaying the goddess and the other deities for the violence and sacrifice of creation. In Norse† mythology, Odin, the chief of the gods, made a kind of self-sacrifice by hanging on the World Tree Yggdrasill for nine days to gain magical knowledge. For this reason, the Norse sometimes sacrificed war captives to Odin by hanging them, and Odin became known as the god of the hanged.

Sacrifice is often an act of worship or obedience. In the book of Genesis in the Bible, God tells Abraham to take his son Isaac to the top of a mountain and sacrifice him. Abraham builds an altar and prepares to sacrifice his son when a voice from heaven tells him to stop, saying, "Now I know that you fear God, because you have not withheld from me your son, your only son." Turning around, Abraham notices a ram caught by its horns in a bush. He releases Isaac and sacrifices the ram instead.

Some myths present sacrifice as a way of setting right the relationship between people and gods. The Kikuyu people of Kenya in eastern Africa tell of a time when no rain fell for three years. The crops dried up, and the people asked their magician what they should do. After performing a magical ceremony, he told them to bring goats to buy a maiden named Wanjiru. The next day everyone gathered around Wanjiru, who began to sink into the ground. When her family tried to help her, those around gave them goats, so the family let her sink. As Wanjiru sank inch by inch into the ground, rain began to fall. By the time she disappeared into the ground, the rain was pouring down. Afterwards, a young warrior who loved Wanjiru went to the place where she had disappeared. Letting himself sink into the underworld, he found Wanjiru, brought her back to the surface, and married her.

Sacrifice may be linked to divination, or foretelling the future. The Druids† of ancient Britain sacrificed both animals and humans in the belief that they could read the future in the victims' dying movements or in the patterns of their intestines. In the story of Sunjata, told by the Mandingo people of Mali in West Africa, a king sacrificed a bull to acknowledge a **prophecy.** A hunter predicted that if the king agreed to marry a hideous young woman, their child would become a great ruler. In Central America, the Mayan Vision Serpent ceremony—held to consult with the dead and determine the future—included offerings of blood drawn from the king. *See also* AZTEC MYTHOLOGY; DRUIDS; ODIN; SUNJATA; YGGDRASILL.

Sagas

The sagas, a rich collection of traditional Scandinavian stories, were written down in Iceland between the late 1100s and the 1300s. They can be divided into several categories: lives of Icelandic kings and bishops, family histories, romances, and sagas of ancient times. This last group of sagas deals with the adventures of legendary heroes. Often set in distant or imaginary locations, they are a major source of information about Norse† mythology.

pagan term used by early Christians to describe non-Christians and non-Christian beliefs

supernatural related to forces beyond the normal world; magical or miraculous

epic long poem about legendary or historical heroes, written in a grand style

Sages

demigod one who is part human and part god

epic long poem about legendary or historical heroes, written in a grand style

patron special guardian, protector, or supporter

First settled in the late 800s by the Vikings—seafaring people from Norway, Sweden, and Denmark—Iceland had a **pagan** culture until about 1000, when Christianity was introduced. One purpose of the sagas was to record the history of the new country and preserve its Viking heritage. The sagas of ancient times include stories about Norse gods such as Thor† and Odin†, who were worshiped by the Vikings, as well as tales about human characters. They treat many of the same mythological themes found in the *Poetic Edda* and the *Prose Edda*—two other key works of Icelandic literature.

The heroes of the sagas of ancient times often undertake dangerous quests to defeat an enemy, seek glory, or win the love of a maiden. Along the way, they may meet an assortment of **supernatural** creatures as well as good and evil people. One of these sagas, the *Völsunga Saga,* closely links the story of a hero named Sigurd to various Norse myths and legends. The saga vividly describes Sigurd's battle with a dragon and his tragic love for the Valkyrie† Brynhild (Brunhilde). Much of the story of the *Völsunga Saga* also appears in the German **epic** the *Nibelungenlied.* **See also** Brunhilde; Nibelungenlied; Norse Mythology; Odin; Sigurd; Thor.

A sage is a wise or holy figure, often an older man, who possesses insight or understanding beyond that of ordinary people. In myths and legends, sages serve as guardians of special knowledge, helpers or advisers to heroes, and examples of wisdom, virtue, and goodness.

Many mythical sages live in deep forests, on mountaintops, or in other places that are withdrawn from the world. Some are divine beings or **demigods.** In Hindu religion and mythology, wise and powerful sages are called *rishis.* The constellation of the Great Bear or Big Dipper in the night sky is said to consist of the seven greatest *rishis.* Other sages appear in Hindu **epics.** According to tradition, a sage named Vyasa, who lived in forests and caves around 1500 B.C., wrote the epic the *Mahabharata.*

Other cultures also have legendary sages in groups of seven, which is considered a sacred or lucky number in many traditions. In China, the Seven Sages of the Bamboo Grove were poets and scholars who abandoned court life for a country retreat. The Seven Sages of Greece were men noted in the ancient Mediterranean world for their wisdom. Among them were a scientist, a lawmaker, and several **patrons** of the arts.

Some legendary sages, such as King Solomon of ancient Israel, became known for their teachings and wise decisions. Solomon's most famous judgment involved two women, both claiming to be the mother of the same baby. Solomon declared that he would settle the dispute by cutting the child in two so that each woman could have half. When one woman offered to give up her claim to spare the child, Solomon knew that she was the true mother. *See also* Seers.

Samson

Samson, who appears in the Old Testament of the Bible, was an exceptionally strong hero of the Israelites of the ancient Near East. According to the story, an angel visited Samson's parents before his birth to tell them they would have a son. The boy was to be raised devoted to God, and he must also refuse all strong drink and never cut his hair.

Samson had tremendous physical strength and led the Israelites against the Philistines†. He performed many remarkable feats, such as killing 1,000 men using only the jawbone of a donkey as a weapon. However, he fell in love with a woman named Delilah, who tricked him into telling her the source of his strength—his long, thick hair. While Samson was asleep one night, Delilah cut off his hair. Samson grew weak and the Philistines seized him. They put out his eyes and chained him to pillars in the temple of their god Dagon. After a time Samson's hair grew back, and his strength returned. During a celebration in the temple, Samson pulled down the pillars to which he was chained. The temple collapsed, killing Samson and all the Philistines inside. **See also** DELILAH.

Santa Claus

dowry money, goods, or property that a woman brings to her husband at marriage

patron special guardian, protector, or supporter

A familiar symbol of Christmas in Europe and North America, Santa Claus is usually pictured as a jolly old man in a red suit who brings gifts to good children. The tradition of Santa Claus is based on a historical figure named St. Nicholas. Nicholas of Bari, the bishop of Myra in Asia Minor (present-day Turkey) in the A.D. 300s, was known for his kindness and generosity. Tales of miracles he performed for the poor and unfortunate grew up around his name. In one story, he provided **dowries** for poor girls who otherwise would not have married.

St. Nicholas became very popular in Europe during the Middle Ages and was adopted as the **patron** saint of Russia. Dutch settlers in America brought his legend with them, and his Dutch name, Sinte Klaas, changed into Santa Claus. His story was combined with northern European tales of a magician who rewarded good children and punished wicked ones. The appearance of Santa Claus was first described in Clement Moore's 1822 poem "The Night Before Christmas," and his image has remained the same to this day. **See also** NICHOLAS, ST.

Satan

adversary enemy; opponent

The Jewish, Christian, and Muslim religions are monotheistic faiths, which means their followers believe there is only one God. That God has a powerful **adversary** known as Satan, or the Devil. Satan's role changed over time, as the three religions developed. At first he was a creature under God's control with the task of testing people's faith. In time, however, Satan came to be seen as the prince of darkness, ruler of all evil spirits, enemy of both God and humankind, and source of treachery and wickedness.

From Adversary to Devil. The name *Satan* comes from a Hebrew word meaning "adversary." It first appears in the Hebrew Bible,

† See **Names and Places** at the end of this volume for further information.

dualistic consisting of two equal and opposing forces

or Old Testament. In the book of Job, God allows this adversary—sometimes called Samael in Jewish literature—to heap misfortunes on Job to see whether Job will turn against God. Judaism was influenced by the **dualistic** Persian religion in which good and evil struggle with each other for control of the universe and for power over human hearts and minds. The Jewish Satan took on some characteristics of Ahriman, the Persian god of evil and ruler of demons.

After about 300 B.C., Satan came to be seen as God's enemy, the source and center of all evil in the world. The serpent that tempted Adam and Eve in Genesis, the first book of the Bible, was identified with Satan. Since that time, artists and writers have often portrayed Satan as a snake or dragon or as a monstrous combination of man and dragon. By the time the books of the Bible known as the New Testament were written, Satan's role as the Devil was well established among Christians.

The Myth of the Fallen Angel. Jewish and Christian traditions offer similar explanations for the Devil's origin. Because God would not create a being of pure evil, Satan was originally an archangel, one of God's most divine or blessed creations. His name is given sometimes as Samael but more often as Lucifer, a bright angel called son of the morning.

Some accounts say that God cast the archangel out of heaven because he would not honor Adam, the first man created by God. When the jealous archangel refused to acknowledge "a lowly thing made of dirt," God punished his pride by throwing him down into hell. There, as Satan, the fallen archangel ruled over a kingdom of devils, former angels who had followed him in his fall.

In Islamic tradition, Satan is known as Shaytan or Iblis. Like the Jewish and Christian Satan, he is a fallen angel who was punished

In many stories, Satan is portrayed as the ruler of evil spirits and the source of all wickedness. This mosaic shows Satan torturing souls in hell.

epic long poem about legendary or historical heroes, written in a grand style

Sati

pyre pile of wood on which a dead body is burned in a funeral ceremony

for refusing to bow down before Adam. But Allah permits Iblis to tempt humans to test their faith.

Other versions of the archangel's fall say that he was thrown out of heaven because of his pride—he dared to compete with God in glory. According to a Hebrew myth, on the third day of creation, Lucifer walked in the Garden of Eden covered with brilliant, glittering jewels set in gold. He had become so filled with pride that he planned to rise above the heavens and become God's equal. God cast Satan down, and his glory turned to darkness and ashes. The Old Testament book of Isaiah describes the archangel's fall:

> How art thou fallen from heaven,
> O Lucifer son of the morning!
> How art thou cast down to the ground,
> Which thou who didst weaken the nations!

Christian legends frequently depict Satan as a tempter who tries to lure the faithful into abandoning their faith. Stories such as the legend of Faust show people making bargains with the Devil. They generally give their souls—for which he is always hungry—in exchange for a gift such as wealth, love, or power. Such bargains always end in terror and despair, unless God steps in to save the poor sinner's soul from Satan.

One of the best-known and most influential literary portraits of Satan can be found in *Paradise Lost,* an **epic** by the English poet John Milton published in 1667. *See also* ADAM AND EVE; AHRIMAN; ANGELS; DEVILS AND DEMONS; FAUST; HEAVEN; HELL; JOB; PERSIAN MYTHOLOGY; SEMITIC MYTHOLOGY; SERPENTS AND SNAKES.

Sati

In Hindu mythology, Sati was the daughter of Daksha, son of the Hindu creator god Brahma. Sati was in love with Shiva, god of destruction, but her father forbade her to have anything to do with him. Her father's objections eventually led Sati to her death.

To find a husband for his daughter, Daksha held a gathering of the gods. Sati was to throw a bouquet of flowers into the air and marry the one who caught it. The only god not invited was Shiva. However, Sati prayed to Shiva, who appeared at the gathering and caught the flowers. Enraged, Daksha had to permit the two to marry.

After Sati's wedding, her father planned a ceremony involving a sacrifice, and again he invited all the gods except Shiva. Unable to persuade her father to invite her husband, Sati threw herself into the sacrificial fire and burned to death. Shiva, overcome by grief, took Sati's body from the flames and began to dance with it. His violent dance threatened to destroy the entire universe. Finally, the god Vishnu† cut Sati's body into pieces, and Shiva ended his dance. According to some versions of the story, Vishnu later brought Sati back to life. The legend of Sati leaping into the fire is sometimes used to explain the Indian tradition of suttee, in which a widow throws herself onto her dead husband's funeral **pyre**. *See also* BRAHMA; HINDUISM AND MYTHOLOGY; SHIVA; VISHNU.

†*See **Names and Places** at the end of this volume for further information.*

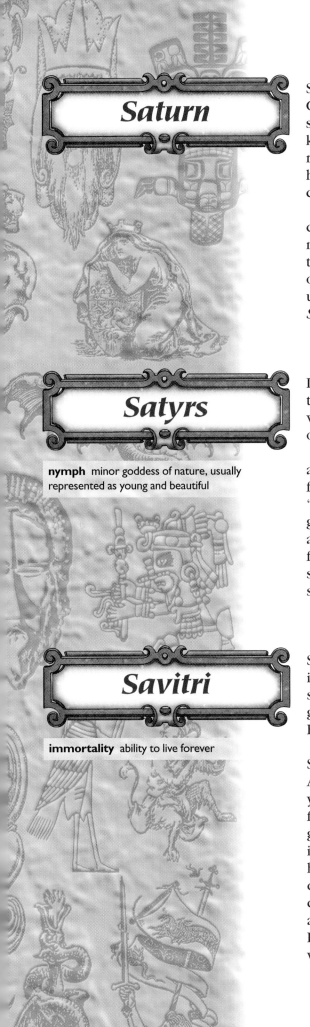

Saturn

Saturn, the Roman god of agriculture, was identified with the Greek god Cronus. In Roman mythology, Saturn fled Greece and settled in Italy after losing a battle with Jupiter†. Saturn became the king of Latium (the area of central Italy that includes Rome) and ruled over a golden age of peace and prosperity. During this time, he taught the people how to plant and tend crops and how to lead civilized lives.

His festival was the Saturnalia, a celebration beginning on December 17 and ending December 25. During Saturnalia, businesses closed, people exchanged presents, and slaves were given the freedom to do and say what they wished. Christians later honored the last day of Saturnalia as the date of the birth of Jesus. Saturn also gave his name to the day of the week known as Saturday. *See also* CRONUS.

Satyrs

nymph minor goddess of nature, usually represented as young and beautiful

In Greek mythology, satyrs were half-man, half-beast creatures that lived in forests and hills. Usually pictured as human above the waist and as horse or goat below the waist, satyrs had pointed ears or horns on their heads.

According to some sources, satyrs were the children of goats and mountain **nymphs.** However, the Greek poet Hesiod† identifies satyrs as brothers of the nymphs, while also calling them "good-for-nothing" and "mischievous." Followers of Dionysus, the god of wine and ecstasy, satyrs had a reputation for drunkenness and lewdness. They were considered symbols of fertility and were frequently portrayed chasing nymphs. During the festival of Dionysus in ancient Athens, satyr plays featuring a chorus of boisterous satyrs were performed along with the tragedies.

Savitri

immortality ability to live forever

Savitri is the name of several figures in Hindu mythology. According to tradition, Savitri is a god of the sun who rides through the sky each day granting long life to humans and **immortality** to the gods. Savitri is also the wife of the god Brahma†; together she and Brahma gave birth to the human race.

Another Hindu legend tells the story of a princess named Savitri. She fell in love with Prince Satyavan, the son of a blind, exiled king. Although a holy man told Savitri that the prince would die within a year, she married him anyway. After a year, Satyavan went into the forest to cut wood, followed by his wife. There they met Yama, the god of death, who began to take the prince away. Touched by Savitri's devotion to her husband, Yama told her that he would grant her anything she wished. First she asked that Satyavan's father recover his sight and his kingdom. Then she asked that she might become the mother of 1,000 children. After Yama agreed, Savitri argued that she could not have children if her husband was dead. Impressed by the way Savitri had tricked him, Yama restored Satyavan to life. *See also* BRAHMA; HINDUISM AND MYTHOLOGY.

25

Scapegoat

ritual ceremony that follows a set pattern

deity god or goddess

Scylla and Charybdis

nymph minor goddess of nature, usually represented as young and beautiful

epic long poem about legendary or historical heroes, written in a grand style

The concept of a scapegoat, a person who is blamed for the sins of others, goes back to ancient times. The term comes from a Hebrew **ritual** that is described in the book of Leviticus in the Old Testament of the Bible. Each year a priest symbolically transferred to a goat the sins of the people of Israel. The goat was thrown over a cliff outside the city of Jerusalem, and its sacrifice was believed to remove the nation's sins. The ritual was originally performed to pacify Azazel, a fallen angel who became a demon of the wilderness.

The Hebrews were not the only group to practice scapegoat rituals. In ancient Athens, two ugly men were chosen as scapegoats during the festival of Thargelia. After dining at a feast, the pair were led through the streets and beaten with branches. Then they were escorted out of town or driven out with stones. The ritual was intended to protect Athens from harm.

The Maya of Central America also held an annual ceremony involving a scapegoat. At the end of each year, Mayan villagers made a clay model of the demon Uuayayah. They placed the model before an image of the **deity** responsible for governing the coming year. Then they carried the model of Uuayayah outside the village to ward off evil.

In Indonesia and the Philippines, scapegoats in the form of boats were used during epidemics to try to rid communities of a disease. The islanders built small boats and loaded them with food and water. They set the boats adrift in the open sea, hoping that the evil spirits that brought the disease would sail away in them. *See also* GREEK MYTHOLOGY; MAYAN MYTHOLOGY; SACRIFICE; SEMITIC MYTHOLOGY.

In Greek mythology, Scylla and Charybdis were a pair of monsters who lived on opposite ends of the Strait of Messina between Italy and Sicily. Scylla was originally a sea **nymph** who was loved by the sea god Poseidon†. Out of jealousy, Poseidon's wife Amphitrite poisoned the waters in which Scylla bathed. This turned Scylla into a six-headed beast with three rows of sharp teeth in each head. When ships passed close by her, she struck out to grab and eat unwary sailors.

Charybdis was also a sea nymph, as well as the daughter of Poseidon. Zeus† transformed her into a dangerous whirlpool across the strait from Scylla. Ships sailing the strait were almost certain to be destroyed by one of the monsters.

In the Greek **epic** the *Odyssey*†, the hero Odysseus lost his ship in Charybdis, but he managed to save himself by clinging to a tree overhanging the water. Later the whirlpool spat up the ship, and Odysseus dropped to safety on its deck. The legend of the two monsters gave birth to the phrase "between Scylla and Charybdis," meaning a situation in which one has to choose between two equally unattractive options. *See also* GREEK MYTHOLOGY; NYMPHS; ODYSSEY, THE.

†See **Names and Places** *at the end of this volume for further information.*

Sebastian, St.

patron special guardian, protector, or supporter
martyr person who suffers or is put to death for a belief

St. Sebastian, the **patron** saint of archers and soldiers, was one of the early **martyrs** of the Christian church. According to legend, Sebastian served in the personal guard of the Roman emperor Diocletian during the late 200s. While in this post Sebastian converted many of his fellow soldiers to Christianity. When Diocletian found out, he had Sebastian shot with arrows.

The archers assumed Sebastian was dead, but he survived and a woman found his body. After she nursed him back to health, Sebastian sought out the emperor and asked him to stop persecuting Christians. Diocletian ordered that Sebastian be beaten to death and thrown into a sewer. His body was recovered and buried near Rome in the Basilica San Sebastiano, which became a popular stop for pilgrims in the Middle Ages. St. Sebastian's feast day is celebrated on January 20.

Sedna

underworld land of the dead
deity god or goddess

In Inuit mythology, the goddess Sedna rules the **underworld** and the creatures of the sea. Myths about Sedna explain the origin of sea creatures and reflect the harsh environment of the Arctic. Because she provides the animals used for food, Sedna is the most important Inuit **deity.**

According to one myth, Sedna was a child with an enormous appetite who tried to eat her father's arm while he was asleep. When he awoke, her father put Sedna in a boat and took her out to sea. He tried to throw her overboard, but she clung tightly to the side of the boat. Her father then chopped off her fingers one joint at a time. As the pieces of Sedna's fingers fell into the water, they turned into whales, seals, and sea lions. When all her fingers were gone, she sank to the bottom of the sea, where she guards the spirits of the dead.

In another version of the story, Sedna was a young woman who refused all the suitors who sought her hand. Then, a seabird disguised as a handsome man visited her and promised that—if she married him—she would live in luxury for the rest of her days. Against her father's wishes, Sedna married the bird. However, she soon found out that the bird's promises had been lies. She led an unhappy existence in a flimsy shelter with only raw fish to eat.

When her father came to visit, Sedna asked him to take her home. Her father killed her husband and set off in his boat with Sedna. However, the other birds stirred up a raging storm on the water. To calm the sea, Sedna's father threw her overboard as an offering to the birds. As in the other tale, she hung on until he cut off her fingers. In some versions of the story, Sedna's father hauled her back into the boat. However, angered by her father's cruelty, she had her dogs try to eat him while he slept. When her father awoke, he cursed himself, Sedna, and her dogs. The ground opened up and swallowed them all, and Sedna became goddess of the underworld. ***See also*** BIRDS IN MYTHOLOGY; NATIVE AMERICAN MYTHOLOGY; UNDERWORLD.

Seers

supernatural related to forces beyond the normal world; magical or miraculous

oracle priest or priestess or other creature through whom a god is believed to speak; also the location (such as a shrine) where such words are spoken

prophet one who claims to have received divine messages or insights

shaman person thought to possess spiritual and healing powers

deity god or goddess

divination act or practice of foretelling the future

omen sign of future events

prophecy foretelling of what is to come; also something that is predicted

ritual ceremony that follows a set pattern

People who claimed special knowledge of the divine or **supernatural** realms have appeared in many myths, legends, folktales, and religious traditions. Those known as seers could see things hidden from others. They had the ability to predict the future or speak for the gods. Others with similar magical gifts have been called diviners, **oracles, prophets,** and **shamans.** They are said to have received special wisdom, power, or understanding from **deities** or spirits, and they have generally had a significant role in religion.

Seers have used various techniques of **divination.** In the ancient world, Babylonian†, Egyptian, and Greek seers often relied on the interpretation of dreams to predict the future, believing dreams to be messages or warnings from the gods. Seers and diviners also explained the significance of events thought to be **omens.** Oracles, such as the famous oracle of Apollo† at Delphi in ancient Greece, were often associated with a particular temple or shrine. They asked questions of the gods on behalf of worshipers or pilgrims and then gave the gods' answers.

Some seers, claiming to be divinely inspired, spoke on a wide range of issues. In the ancient Near East, prophets and diviners frequently became involved in politics. Hebrew prophets such as Samuel, Elijah, and Amos did not merely foretell the future. They also gave their views on religious practices and social conditions that they believed were wrong.

Several seers mentioned in Greek myths were associated with Apollo. Mopsus, a seer who took part in the quest for the Golden Fleece†, was sometimes said to be a son of Apollo. The seer Laocoön was a priest of Apollo until he broke his vow by fathering children. The best-known seer of Greek mythology was Tiresias, who had been blinded by the gods. According to some stories, Zeus† gave him the power of **prophecy** to make up for his loss of sight.

The Druids, priests of an ancient Celtic† religion, were said to be seers and magicians. Like the prophets of the ancient Near East, they sometimes held political power as advisers to rulers. The Druid Cathbadh, who advised King Conchobhar of Ulster in Ireland, foresaw the destruction of the kingdom. Druidic ceremonies of divination included human and animal sacrifice.

In Norse† mythology, the seer Mimir guarded a sacred spring at a root of the World Tree, Yggdrasill. Odin† gained magical knowledge by drinking from the spring, but he had to pay for it by giving one of his eyes to Mimir. The Norse goddess Freyja was also a seer. She introduced the gods to the type of divination called *seid,* which involved going into a trance and answering questions about the future.

The ceremonies described in Norse myths are similar to some of the **rituals** performed by traditional Siberian and Native American shamans. Shamans were believed to have the power to communicate with or travel to the spirit world. Generally, they did so for the purpose of healing rather than for predicting the future. Sometimes spirits spoke through shamans. According to the Haida of the Pacific Northwest of North America, the spirit Lagua used a shaman to teach them how to use iron.

† See **Names and Places** at the end of this volume for further information.

demigod one who is part human and part god

deity god or goddess

city-state independent state consisting of a city and its surrounding territory

Hindu mythology includes many wise and holy men called seers or sages. They possess great spiritual power as a result of living pure and simple lives. A few seers are considered **demigods,** born from the thoughts of the god Brahma†. Often, Hindu wise men are the teachers of kings or heroes. Although generally virtuous, some display pride or anger. One myth tells of Visvamitra, a proud seer whose standards were so high and whose demands so great that he destroyed his king. *See also* CASSANDRA; DELPHI; DRUIDS; FREYJA; LAOCOÖN; MIMIR; SAGES; TIRESIAS.

Semitic Mythology

Semitic mythology arose among several cultures that flourished in the ancient Near East, a region that extended from Mesopotamia† in modern Iraq to the eastern coast of the Mediterranean Sea. These groups of people spoke Semitic languages, had similar religions, and worshiped related **deities.** Three great religions—Judaism, Christianity, and Islam—grew out of Semitic traditions.

Semitic peoples shared many of the same myths and legends. Among their major gods and goddesses were those responsible for creation, fertility, death, and the afterlife. The names of the deities varied slightly from culture to culture. Common themes of Semitic myths included the creation of the world, a great flood, and a hero who overcame a challenge. Some themes, such as the death and rebirth of fertility gods, were rooted in the agricultural way of life of these Near Eastern peoples.

Origins. Between about 3000 and 300 B.C., ancient Mesopotamia was home to a series of civilizations, beginning with the Sumerians, who built the first **city-states.** The Sumerians lived in the southern part of the region between the Tigris and Euphrates Rivers. They were followed by the Akkadians, who settled to the north, the Babylonians, and the Assyrians. Later, Sumer and Akkad became known as Babylonia. The Assyrians settled even farther north along the Tigris.

The Sumerians did not speak a Semitic language. However, the Akkadians and other Semitic peoples who later rose to power in Mesopotamia adopted many parts of Sumerian culture, mythology, and religion. This Sumerian influence shaped thinking and storytelling in the region for thousands of years.

One of the central Sumerian myths, the story of Inanna and Dumuzi, shows how part of the ancient mythology survived in later cultures. Inanna, goddess of light, life, and fertility, was ready to choose a husband. Two men wanted to marry her—Enkimdu, a farmer, and Dumuzi, a shepherd. Inanna leaned toward Enkimdu, but Dumuzi told her that his flocks and herds of livestock could produce more wealth than could Enkimdu's fields. The rivals competed for Inanna's hand until Enkimdu withdrew. Enkimdu then allowed Dumuzi to graze his flocks on his land, and in turn Dumuzi invited Enkimdu to attend his wedding to the goddess. The rivalry between the farmer and the herder in this myth is echoed in the Jewish story of Cain and Abel. Some historians of mythology

29

Semitic Deities

Deity	Role
Adad, Ishkur, Addu, Hadad	Assyrian and Babylonian god of storms and weather
Allah	single, all-powerful God of Islam
Anat	Canaanite goddess of fertility, love, and war
Anu, An	chief creator and sky god
Ashur	main god of Assyria, warrior god
Baal	Canaanite god associated with rain and fertility
Dagon, Dagan	god associated with fertility, vegetation, and military strength
El, Elohim	Canaanite father of the gods, most high judge, creator god
Enki, Ea	creator god associated with water, storms, and wisdom
Enlil	god of creation, wind, land, and the sea
Ishtar, Inanna, Astarte	mother goddess of light, life, fertility, and love
Marduk	chief god of the Babylonians
Shamash	sun god
Yahweh	single, all-powerful God of Judaism

underworld land of the dead

believe that such tales grew out of ancient social tensions between settled agricultural communities and roving groups of livestock herders.

Over time Inanna became known by her Akkadian name, Ishtar. Dumuzi also acquired other names—the people of early Israel called him Tammuz. One widespread story about Inanna and Dumuzi says that Inanna descended into the **underworld** and became a corpse there. The gods managed to restore her to life, but Dumuzi had to go to the underworld as her substitute. He came to be seen as a god of vegetation who had to die and be reborn each year. Many later myths about dying gods, including that of Adonis in Greek mythology, resemble the story of Inanna and Dumuzi.

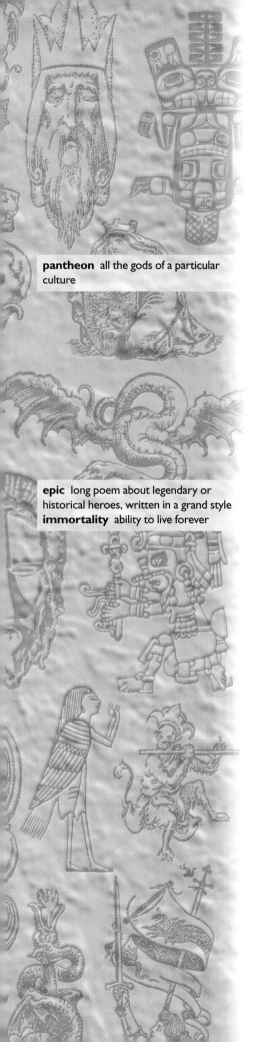

Another basic Semitic myth that came from Sumer is the story of a flood that covered the earth after humans angered the gods. Warned by the gods (or God) to build a boat, one righteous man—such as Noah—and his family survived the flood to give humankind a new start.

Mesopotamian Mythology. The myths of the Akkadians, Babylonians, and Assyrians depicted a world full of mysterious spiritual powers that could threaten humans. People dreaded demons and ghosts and used magical spells for protection against them. They worshiped a **pantheon** of a dozen or so major deities and many other minor gods.

All Mesopotamian peoples honored a fertility goddess such as Inanna or Ishtar. They also recognized three creator gods, called An, Enlil, and Enki by the Sumerians and Anu, Enlil, and Ea by the Akkadians, Babylonians, and Assyrians. An was the chief of the gods. Enlil was a god of wind and land who could be destructive, and Enki was usually associated with water, wisdom, and the arts of civilization. The moon god, known as Sin or Nanna, appeared in a myth in which demons tried to devour him. The powerful god Marduk stopped the demons before they could finish the job. The moon god grew to his former size and repeated that growth every month, marking the passage of time.

The best-known Mesopotamian myth is the Babylonian **epic** of Gilgamesh, the story of a hero king's search for **immortality.** A bold and brave warrior, Gilgamesh performed many extraordinary feats during his journey. Although he failed to obtain his goal—the secret of eternal life—he gained greater wisdom about how to make his life meaningful.

Another legend that deals with the question of why humans die is the myth of Adapa, the first human being. The water god Ea formed Adapa out of mud. Although Adapa was mortal, Ea's touch gave him divine strength and wisdom.

pantheon all the gods of a particular culture

epic long poem about legendary or historical heroes, written in a grand style
immortality ability to live forever

In a story from Mesopotamian mythology, Zu, a bird god from the underworld, stole the tablets that provided control over the universe. On this stone tablet from around 2200 B.C., Zu stands before the water god Ea for judgment.

patron special guardian, protector, or supporter

The Invisible Queen

To the ancient Mesopotamians, light and darkness, life and death, were two halves of a whole. Inanna, the goddess of heaven, ruled the living world, and her sister Ereshkigal, or darkness, was queen of the dead. Neither sister could exist without the other—together they made existence complete. But while Inanna lived in the world that could be seen by humans, Ereshkigal was invisible. Mesopotamian artists never portrayed Ereshkigal directly, but they did create images of the monsters and demons that Ereshkigal sent to trouble the living.

One day, when Adapa was fishing, the wind overturned his boat. Adapa cursed the wind. According to one version of the story, the wind was in the form of a bird, and Adapa tore off its wings. The high god Anu called Adapa to heaven to explain his actions. Adapa asked his father, Ea, for advice on how to act in heaven. Ea told him to wear mourning clothes, to be humble, and to refuse food and drink because they would kill him. So when Anu offered food, Adapa declined it. Unfortunately, Ea's advice had been mistaken. The food Adapa rejected was the food of immortality that would have allowed human beings to live forever. Adapa's choice meant that all men and women must die.

Mythology was closely interwoven with political power in ancient Mesopotamia. Monarchs were believed to rule by the will of the gods and were responsible for maintaining good relations between the heavenly world and their kingdoms. Each of the early city-states had as its **patron** one of the deities of the pantheon, and the importance of the god rose and fell with the fortunes of its city. A main theme of *Enuma Elish,* the Babylonian creation epic, is the rise of Marduk, the patron god of Babylon. Marduk became a leader of the gods, just as Babylon rose to power in the region.

Marduk appears again in a Babylonian myth about Zu, a bird god from the underworld. A frequent enemy of the other gods, Zu stole the tablets that gave Enlil control over the universe. When the high god Anu asked for a volunteer to attack Zu, several gods refused because of Zu's new power. Finally, Marduk took on Zu, defeated him, and recovered the tablets. This restored the universe to its proper order.

Canaanite Mythology. The Canaanites were Semitic peoples who occupied the lands along the eastern coast of the Mediterranean Sea. Canaanite culture flourished in the city of Ugarit, on the Syrian coast, between 1500 and 1200 B.C. Their culture was continued by the Phoenicians, who settled south of Ugarit and later established a colony at Carthage in what is now Tunisia.

The chief of the Ugaritic pantheon was El, the father of the gods, who was generally portrayed as a wise old man. Baal, an active and powerful deity, was associated with fertility and sometimes identified with the storm god Adad. Ashera, the mother of the gods, was the wife of El.

Baal appears in a set of Ugaritic myths called the Baal cycle. These stories describe Baal's rise to power and the challenges he faced from other deities and powerful forces. An underlying theme of the Baal cycle is the tension between the old god El and the young and vigorous Baal. Although El remained supreme, Baal became a king among the gods. He defeated Yam, also called Leviathan, who represented the destructive force of nature and was associated with the sea or with floods. Baal also had to make peace with his sister Anat, a goddess of fertility, who conducted a bloody sacrifice of warriors. Finally, Baal and Anat went to the underworld to confront Mot, the god of death. El presided over the battle between Baal and Mot. Neither god won.

Baal, one of the most widely worshiped gods in ancient Canaan, was associated with fertility and rain. His cult spread to other people in the ancient Near East, including the Egyptians, Babylonians, and Assyrians. This statue of Baal dates from the 1300s B.C.

Other Ugaritic myths deal with legendary kings. Although these tales may have some basis in historical fact, the details are lost. One legend told the story of King Keret, who longed for a son. In a dream, El told Keret to take the princess of a neighboring kingdom as his wife. Promising to honor Anat and Ashera, the king did so, and his new wife bore seven sons and a daughter. However, Keret became ill and neglected the worship of the goddesses. Only a special ceremony to Baal could restore the king's health and the health of the kingdom. This myth illustrates the Semitic belief that the gods sent good or ill fortune to the people through the king.

Jewish Mythology. The ancient Israelites were a Semitic people who settled in Canaan. In time, they established the kingdoms of Israel and Judah, where the modern nation of Israel is today. In 722 B.C., the Assyrians gained control of the kingdom of Israel. The Babylonians conquered Judah in 586 B.C., destroying the city of Jerusalem and removing its inhabitants to Babylon for some years. Eventually the people of Judah came to be known as Jews.

Over the years the Jews produced sacred books, some of which form the Tanach, a set of documents known to Christians as the Old Testament of the Bible. These books include myths and legends about the history of the early Israelites as well as information about their religious beliefs. Traditional Jewish stories were influenced by ancient Semitic mythology. Connections are clearly seen in such stories as the fight between Cain and Abel and the great flood survived by Noah in his ark. In the same way, the story of creation in the book of Genesis in the Old Testament contains parallels to Mesopotamian myths about how Marduk organized the universe. One major difference between Jewish tradition and earlier Semitic mythology, however, is that Judaism was and is **monotheistic.** Instead of a pantheon of deities, it referred to a single, all-powerful God, sometimes called Yahweh.

As Judaism developed over the centuries, new stories, sacred books, and commentary emerged to expand on the ancient texts. The term midrash refers to this large body of Jewish sacred literature, including a vast number of myths, legends, fables, and stories that date from the **medieval** era or earlier. These narratives are called the Haggadah, or "telling," and they are cherished as both instruction and entertainment.

Sometimes the Haggadah fills in the gaps that exist in older narratives. For example, Genesis contains an account of how Cain

monotheistic believing in only one god

medieval relating to the Middle Ages in Europe, a period from about A.D. 500 to 1500

Semitic Mythology

Other entries relating to Semitic mythology include

Adad	Balaam	Inanna	Nimrod
Adam and Eve	Cain and Abel	Ishtar	Noah
Anat	Dagon	Jezebel	Samson
Anu	Delilah	Job	Shamash
Ariel	Eden, Garden of	Jonah	Sheba, Queen of
Ark of the Covenant	El	Leviathan	Sheol
Armageddon	Enkidu	Lilith	Sodom and Gomorrah
Ashur	Enlil	Marduk	Telepinu
Baal	Enuma Elish	Moloch	Tiamat
Babel, Tower of	Gilgamesh	Nabu	Utnapishtim

prophet one who claims to have received divine messages or insights
patriarch man who is the founder or oldest member of a group

murdered Abel. The Haggadah adds the information that no one knew what to do with Abel's body, for his was the first death that humans had witnessed. Adam, the father of Cain and Abel, saw a raven dig a hole in the ground and bury a dead bird, and he decided to bury Abel in the same way.

Jewish tradition influenced Christianity, a monotheistic faith that began as an offshoot of Judaism. The two religions share many sacred stories and texts. The Tanach, especially the books of Genesis and Exodus, contains stories that are part of Christianity—God's creation of the earth, Adam and Eve in the Garden of Eden, Noah and the flood, and Moses and the Exodus. However, the New Testament of the Bible, which deals with the life and works of Jesus, is unique to Christianity.

Islamic Mythology. Like Christianity, Islam is a monotheistic Semitic faith that developed from Jewish traditions. Islam dates from A.D. 622, when an Arab named Muhammad declared himself to be the **prophet** of God, or Allah. Islamic tradition recognizes Abraham, Noah, Moses, and other ancient **patriarchs** of Judaism as earlier prophets. Muslims, followers of Islam, also believe that Jesus was a prophet.

The word of Allah as made known to Muhammad is contained in the Islamic sacred text, the Qur'an or Koran. As time passed, Muslim scholars and teachers all over the Islamic world added more information about Muhammad and his followers as well as interpretations of Islamic law and the sayings of the prophet. They incorporated elements of Semitic, Persian, and Greek mythology or stories about Muhammad, his family, and other key figures in Islamic history.

Although such storytelling was not officially part of Islam—and was sometimes vigorously discouraged by Islamic authorities—it appealed to many Muslims. As Islam spread to new areas, local traditions and legends became mingled with the basic Islamic beliefs.

In Pakistan, for example, old folk tales about girls dying of love came to be seen as symbols of souls longing to be united with Allah.

Many of the legends surrounding Muhammad credit him with miraculous events. Some tales say that Muhammad cast no shadow or that when he was about to eat poisoned meat, the food itself warned him not to taste it. According to legend, the angel Gabriel guided Muhammad, who rode a winged horse called Buraq or Borak, on a mystical journey through heaven, where he met the other prophets.

Similarly, historical figures who founded mystical Islamic brotherhoods came to be associated with stories of miracles, such as riding on lions and curing the sick. In some cases, these legends have elements of traditional myths about pre-Islamic deities or heroes. Romantic tales about Alexander the Great may have colored some of the tales about Khir, an Islamic mythical figure and the patron of travelers, who is said to have been a companion of Moses. ***See also*** DEVILS AND DEMONS; FLOODS; PERSIAN MYTHOLOGY; SATAN; SCAPEGOAT.

Serpents and Snakes

This Norse brooch of the 600s shows Jormungand, the serpent that encircles the world in Norse mythology. In one story, the god Thor tries to drain the ocean and remove the World Serpent.

immortality ability to live forever

underworld land of the dead

Serpents and snakes play a role in many of the world's myths and legends. Sometimes these mythic beasts appear as ordinary snakes. At other times, they take on magical or monstrous forms. Serpents and snakes have long been associated with good as well as with evil, representing both life and death, creation and destruction.

Serpents and Snakes as Symbols. In religion, mythology, and literature, serpents and snakes often stand for fertility or a creative life force—partly because the creatures can be seen as symbols of the male sex organ. They have also been associated with water and earth because many kinds of snakes live in the water or in holes in the ground. The ancient Chinese connected serpents with life-giving rain. Traditional beliefs in Australia, India, North America, and Africa have linked snakes with rainbows, which in turn are often related to rain and fertility.

As snakes grow, many of them shed their skin at various times, revealing a shiny new skin underneath. For this reason snakes have become symbols of rebirth, transformation, **immortality,** and healing. The ancient Greeks considered snakes sacred to Asclepius, the god of medicine. He carried a caduceus, a staff with one or two serpents wrapped around it, which has become the symbol of modern physicians.

For both the Greeks and the Egyptians, the snake represented eternity. Ouroboros, the Greek symbol of eternity, consisted of a snake curled into a circle or hoop, biting its own tail. The Ouroboros grew out of the belief that serpents eat themselves and are reborn from themselves in an endless cycle of destruction and creation.

Living on and in the ground, serpents came to be seen in some religions and mythologies as guardians of the **underworld.** In this role they could represent hidden wisdom or sacred mysteries, but they also had other, more sinister meanings. The use of serpents

Snakes appear in the myths and legends of the Aborigines of Australia. This wall painting located near the town of Kuranda, Queensland, shows a snake among many different animals.

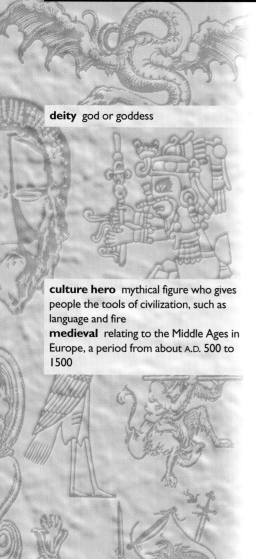

deity god or goddess

culture hero mythical figure who gives people the tools of civilization, such as language and fire

medieval relating to the Middle Ages in Europe, a period from about A.D. 500 to 1500

as symbols of death, evil, or treachery may be related to the fact that some of them are poisonous and dangerous. Satan and other devils have frequently been portrayed as snakes, as in the biblical story of Eden where a sly serpent tempts Eve and Adam into disobeying God. Some Christian saints are said to have driven away snakes as a sign of miraculous powers given to them by God. According to legend, St. Patrick cleared Ireland of snakes.

The Nagas of Hindu and Buddhist mythology show how serpents can symbolize both good and evil, hopes and fears. Although these snake gods could take any shape, including a fully human one, they often appeared as human heads on serpent bodies. The Nagas lived in underwater or underground kingdoms. They controlled rainfall and interacted with **deities** and humans in a variety of ways. Some were good, such as Muchalinda, the snake king who shielded Buddha from a storm. Others could be cruel and vengeful.

Serpents and Snakes in Myths. Many mythical creatures, such as dragons, combine snakelike qualities with features of humans or animals. In Greek mythology, Echidna was a half-woman, half-serpent monster whose offspring included several dragons. Cecrops had a man's head and chest on a snake's body and was a **culture hero** to the Athenians. In Toltec and Aztec mythology, Quetzalcoatl, the Feathered Serpent, held an important place. In **medieval** Europe, people told tales of the basilisk, a serpent with a dragon's body that could kill merely by looking at or breathing on its victims. Melusina, another figure in European folklore, was part woman, part fish and snake and had to spend one day each week in water.

Myths that emphasized the frightening or evil aspects of serpents and snakes often portrayed them as the enemies of deities and humans. The Greek hero Perseus rescued Andromeda, who was chained to a rock, by slaying a sea monster that threatened to eat her. In Norse† mythology, a monster called the Midgard serpent—also known as Jormungand—was wrapped around the earth, biting its tail. Thor† battled the serpent, which lived in the sea, where its movements caused storms around the world. Another Norse monster, the Nidhogg or dread biter, was an evil serpent coiled around one of the roots of Yggdrasill, the World Tree. It was forever trying to destroy the tree by biting or squeezing it.

†*See **Names and Places** at the end of this volume for further information.*

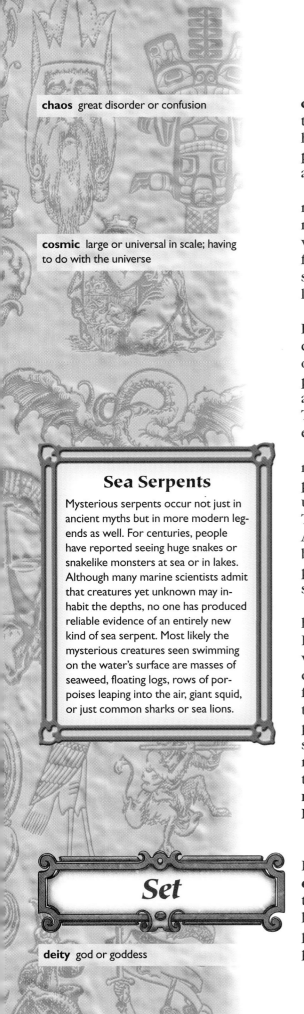

chaos great disorder or confusion

cosmic large or universal in scale; having to do with the universe

Sea Serpents

Mysterious serpents occur not just in ancient myths but in more modern legends as well. For centuries, people have reported seeing huge snakes or snakelike monsters at sea or in lakes. Although many marine scientists admit that creatures yet unknown may inhabit the depths, no one has produced reliable evidence of an entirely new kind of sea serpent. Most likely the mysterious creatures seen swimming on the water's surface are masses of seaweed, floating logs, rows of porpoises leaping into the air, giant squid, or just common sharks or sea lions.

Set

deity god or goddess

In the mythology of ancient Egypt, Apopis was a demon of **chaos** who appeared in the form of a serpent. Each night he attacked Ra†, the sun god. But Mehen, another huge serpent, coiled himself around Ra's sun boat to protect the god from Apopis—a perfect illustration of how snakes can be symbols of both good and evil in mythology.

Mythological snakes that act as forces of good have various roles, such as creating the world, protecting it, or helping humans. Stories of the Fon people of West Africa tell of Da, a serpent whose 3,500 coils support the **cosmic** ocean in which the earth floats. Another 3,500 of its coils support the sky. Humans occasionally catch a glimpse of many-colored Da in a rainbow or in light reflected on the surface of water.

The Aboriginal people of northern Australia tell how the Great Rainbow Snake Julunggul shaped the world. When human blood dropped into a waterhole, Julunggul grew angry. He sent a wave of water washing across the earth, and he swallowed people, plants, and animals. Julunggul reared up toward heaven, but an ant spirit bit him and made him vomit up what he had swallowed. This happened again and again until Julunggul departed from the earth, leaving people, plants, and animals in all parts of it.

According to a story of the Diegueño Indians of California, humans obtained many of the secrets of civilization from a huge serpent named Umai-hulhlya-wit. This serpent lived in the ocean until people performed a ceremony and called him onto the land. They built an enclosure for him, but it was too small to hold him. After Umai-hulhlya-wit had squeezed as much of himself as possible into the enclosure, the people set him on fire. Soon the serpent's body exploded, showering the earth with the knowledge, secrets, songs, and other cultural treasures he had contained.

Hindu myths contain many tales of serpents. Kaliya was a five-headed serpent king who poisoned water and land until the god Krishna defeated him in battle. Kaliya then worshiped Krishna, who spared his life. Kadru was a snake goddess who bore 1,000 children. Legend says that they still live today as snakes in human form. One of Kadru's children was the world snake Shesha that the gods used to turn a mountain and stir up the ocean, just as people churn milk into butter by using a rope coiled around a stick or paddle. As the gods churned the ocean with the snake, many precious things arose from it, including the moon, a magical tree, and the Amrita, or water of life. *See also* ADAM AND EVE; ANIMALS IN MYTHOLOGY; ASCLEPIUS; BASILISK; CADUCEUS; DRAGONS; HYDRA; MEDUSA; NAGAS; PATRICK, ST.; QUETZALCOATL; SATAN.

In Egyptian mythology Set (or Seth) was the evil brother of the **deities** Osiris, Isis, and Nephthys. The son of the earth god Geb and the sky goddess Nut, Set tore himself from his mother's body before he was fully formed. For this reason, he used pieces of animals to complete his body. Among the many animals associated with Set were the pig, donkey, scorpion, antelope, hippopotamus, and crocodile.

37

cult group bound together by devotion to a particular person, belief, or god

underworld land of the dead

resurrect to raise from the dead

Shakuntala

epic long poem about legendary or historical heroes, written in a grand style

nymph minor goddess of nature, usually represented as young and beautiful

Originally a sky and storm god, Set was highly regarded at first, and his **cult** was one of the oldest in Egypt. Each day he rode across the sky in the sun ship of the great god Ra†; each night as he traveled through the **underworld,** he killed the mighty serpent Aapep to protect Ra. In time, however, Set became jealous of the other gods, and his treachery against them turned him into one of the chief forces of evil.

Above all, Set envied his brother Osiris, who ruled as king of Egypt while Set served only as lord of the desert. Determined to destroy his brother, Set arranged a great feast to which he invited Osiris and the other gods. He had carpenters construct a large and magnificently decorated box, which he placed at the entrance hall of his palace. When Osiris arrived, Set tricked him into getting inside the box. As soon as Osiris stepped into the box, Set ordered his servants to nail down the lid, seal it with molten lead, and throw it into the Nile River. Osiris drowned.

Their sister Isis, who was also Osiris's wife, searched for her husband and eventually found the box. She brought Osiris back to life long enough to conceive a son, Horus. However, Set found Osiris's body and cut it into pieces. Then he scattered the pieces throughout Egypt. Nephthys, Set's wife and sister, helped Isis locate the pieces and **resurrect** Osiris. After that, Osiris went to rule the underworld as king of the dead.

Horus later fought Set to avenge his father's death. In a series of great battles, Horus defeated his evil uncle. He would have killed him except that Isis took pity on Set and asked Horus to spare his life. Ancient Egyptians viewed the battle between Horus and Set as the ultimate struggle between good and evil.

As the cult of Osiris grew in Egypt, worship of Set declined. Eventually, Egyptian priests declared Set to be an enemy of the gods. His name and image were removed from many monuments, and he became associated with Aapep (known also as Apopis), the monstrous serpent that he had once defeated each night to protect Ra. *See also* EGYPTIAN MYTHOLOGY; HORUS; ISIS; NUT; OSIRIS; RA (RE); SERPENTS AND SNAKES.

Shakuntala is the heroine of a great love story told in the Hindu **epic** the *Mahabharata*. She was the daughter of a wise man named Vishvamitra and the **nymph** Menaka, who abandoned her in the forest as an infant. A hermit who lived in the woods found the child and raised her as his daughter.

One day, King Dushyanta was hunting and stopped at the hermit's home. When the king saw Shakuntala, he fell in love with her and the two were married. The king returned to his palace and Shakuntala stayed behind. She soon gave birth to a son, Bharata.

Some time later, Shakuntala took the boy to the palace to meet his father. However, Dushyanta did not recognize her. As the mother and child stood before the king, a voice from heaven told him that the boy was indeed his son. Prompted by the voice, Dushyanta remembered Shakuntala, proclaimed her to be his

†*See **Names and Places** at the end of this volume for further information.*

queen, and named Bharata the heir to his throne. Bharata became the ancestor of the two great families that are featured in the *Mahabharata.*

In some versions of the legend, Dushyanta failed to recognize Shakuntala because she had lost a ring he had given her; he accepted her when the ring was found. The Indian playwright Kālidāsa based his most famous drama on the story. *See also* HINDUISM AND MYTHOLOGY; MAHABHARATA, THE.

Shalott, The Lady of

joust fight on horseback between two knights

In the Arthurian legends†, the Lady of Shalott was a young woman named Elaine of Astolat who died of unfulfilled love for Sir Lancelot, the greatest of King Arthur's knights. Lancelot had entered a **jousting** tournament but wanted to hide his true identity, so he asked Elaine to give him a different shield. In return, he agreed to wear her colors in the tournament.

Lancelot won the contest, but he was injured and fled to avoid being discovered. Elaine found him and nursed him back to health. She also revealed her love for him. However, Lancelot could not return her affections because he loved Guinevere.

The heartbroken Elaine died of grief, but before dying, she wrote a letter to Lancelot requesting that he bury her. Her father placed the letter in her hand and put her body on a barge, which a mute boatman rowed to King Arthur's court at Camelot. Lancelot saw the barge and recognized Elaine. When King Arthur read Elaine's letter, he asked Lancelot to bury her, thus granting her final request. *See also* ARTHURIAN LEGENDS; LANCELOT.

Shamash

pantheon all the gods of a particular culture

underworld land of the dead

epic long poem about legendary or historical heroes, written in a grand style
immortality ability to live forever

Shamash was the sun god in the mythology of the ancient Near East. Associated with truth, justice, and healing, he was one of the most active gods in the **pantheons** of ancient Sumer†, Babylonia†, and Assyria†.

The son of the Sumerian moon god Sin, Shamash was the brother of the goddess Ishtar. His wife Aya (youth) bore him four sons—Giru (fire), Kittum (truth), Mesharum (justice), and Nusku (light). As god of the sun, Shamash moved across the sky during the day, and according to some legends, he moved through the **underworld** during the night. In other stories, the god and his sons crossed the sky in a chariot by day and rested in a palace on a mountain at night.

Shamash was responsible for maintaining the order of the universe. Nothing could hide from his bright light, which banished darkness and revealed lies. The defender of the poor and the weak, he was the enemy of evil.

In the Babylonian **epic** of Gilgamesh, Shamash offered the hero help and advice in carrying out a dangerous quest for **immortality.** In ancient art, Shamash was usually shown as a disk or wheel, although sometimes he appeared as a king holding a staff of justice and a wheel of truth. *See also* GILGAMESH; ISHTAR; SEMITIC MYTHOLOGY; SUN.

39

Sheba, Queen of

Both Jewish and African traditions include stories about the Queen of Sheba. The ruler of a wealthy nation in southern Arabia, the queen had heard tales about the great wisdom of Solomon, king of the Hebrews. Curious, she decided to go to Jerusalem to meet him.

According to the book of Kings in the Bible, the queen arrived in Jerusalem and asked King Solomon a series of difficult questions. He responded wisely to each one. The queen presented Solomon with many gifts and returned to her home.

In an African version of the story, the Queen of Sheba is an Ethiopian ruler named Makeda. She traveled to Jerusalem to visit Solomon. She was so impressed by his wisdom that she gave up her religion and adopted Judaism. After six months, Makeda told Solomon she wanted to return home. The king gave her a ring to remember him. He also told her that if she became pregnant and had a male child, her child would become king of Ethiopia.

Nine months later, Makeda bore a son whom she named Menelik. When Menelik was a young man, she sent him to Jerusalem to visit his father. Solomon recognized the young man as his son because of the resemblance between them. Solomon embraced and blessed Menelik, who became the king of Ethiopia and the legendary ancestor of later Ethiopian kings. *See also* AFRICAN MYTHOLOGY; SEMITIC MYTHOLOGY.

Piero Della Francesca's painting of the mid-1450s illustrates the meeting of the Queen of Sheba and King Solomon in Jerusalem.

Sheol

According to Hebrew tradition, Sheol—which means the pit—was a realm beneath the earth where the spirits of the dead resided. It was in many ways the opposite of the world of the living. While light shone on the earth, darkness veiled Sheol. On earth the living had solid bodies, but in Sheol the dead existed as shadows.

The souls of all people went to Sheol, regardless of their behavior during life. As a result, it was not considered a place of punishment for wickedness. In fact, a person who was properly mourned by his relatives after death was believed to join his ancestors in Sheol. In some accounts the souls in Sheol slept, while in others they experienced hopelessness or fear. ***See also* AFTERLIFE; HELL; SEMITIC MYTHOLOGY; UNDERWORLD.**

Shiva

Shiva, the destroyer, is one of the three supreme gods in Hindu mythology. The other two are Brahma, the creator, and Vishnu, the preserver. Shiva's destructive powers are awesome, but they also have a positive side in that destruction usually leads to new forms of existence. In art, Shiva is often portrayed with four arms, four faces, and three eyes. A glance from the third eye in the center of his forehead has the power to destroy anything in creation, including humans and gods. In the Vedas, a collection of ancient sacred texts, Shiva is identified with the storm god Rudra.

Birth of Shiva. According to one myth, Shiva first appeared when Brahma and Vishnu were arguing about which of them was more powerful. Their argument was interrupted by the sudden appearance of a great blazing pillar whose roots and branches extended beyond view into the earth and sky. Brahma became a goose and flew up to find the top of the pillar, while Vishnu turned into a boar and dug into the earth to look for its roots. Unsuccessful in their search, the two gods returned and saw Shiva emerge from an opening in the pillar. Recognizing Shiva's great power, they accepted him as the third ruler of the universe.

Roles and Powers. Shiva is a complex god with many roles and powers. In his destroyer role, he often haunts cemeteries, wearing a headdress of snakes and a necklace of skulls. A band of terrifying demons, hungering for blood, accompanies him.

Yet despite his destructiveness, Shiva can be helpful to humans and other gods. He acts as a divine judge who shows no mercy to the wicked. He gains spiritual strength from periods of meditation—deep thought—in the Himalayas. When he dances, he represents truth, and by dancing he banishes ignorance and helps relieve the suffering of his followers. According to one myth, Shiva saved the gods and the world from destruction by swallowing the poison of Vasuki, a serpent the gods used to produce the water of life. Drinking the poison made Shiva's neck blue, and he is often shown that way in art.

One of Shiva's greatest services to the world was to tame the sacred Ganges River, which flows from the Himalayas. At one time,

the Ganges passed only through the heavens, leaving the earth dry. After a wise man changed the course of the river, it became a raging torrent and threatened to flood the earth. Shiva stood beneath the river and let its waters wind through his hair to calm its flow.

In another story, the gods were threatened by demons and asked Shiva for help. He agreed—on the condition that the gods lend him some of their own strength. However, after defeating the demons, Shiva refused to return the borrowed strength. As a result, he became the most powerful being in the universe. Shiva also has many weapons that make him unbeatable, including a club with a skull on the end, a sword and spear made from thunderbolts, and a bow made from a rainbow. *See also* BRAHMA; HINDUISM AND MYTHOLOGY; SATI; VEDAS; VISHNU.

Siberian Mythology

Siberia is a vast region in northern Asia, stretching from the Ural Mountains in the west to the Pacific Ocean in the east. To the north lies the Arctic Ocean; to the south lie Mongolia, China, and Central Asia. European Russians have been settling in Siberia for several centuries, but the region's original inhabitants were hunting, fishing, and herding peoples whose cultures were related to those of other northern groups, such as the Inuit of North America. Siberian mythology and religion reflected a world in which humans depended on and respected animals, believing that the animals had spirits and could change form.

Elements of Mythology. Traditionally, Siberians viewed the world as the middle realm—or region—in a series of three, five, or seven worlds that were stacked one on top of the other. As in many belief systems, the realms above belonged to good gods and spirits, those below to evil ones. A tree connected the worlds of Siberian myths in the same way that the World Tree Yggdrasill linked realms in Norse† mythology. The tree's roots and branches extended into all levels.

Shamans held a central role in Siberian religion and mythology. They were believed to travel between worlds by climbing the World Tree or by flying, and they communicated with the spirit world through ceremonies and trances. The healing magic of shamans involved finding or curing the lost or damaged souls of sick people.

Many Siberian myths deal with powerful shamans. The Buriat people of the Lake Baikal region told of Morgon-Kara, who could bring the dead back to life. This angered the lord of the dead, who complained to the high god of heaven. The high god tested the shaman by sealing a man's soul in a bottle. Riding his magic drum into the spirit universe, Morgon-Kara found the soul in the bottle. Turning himself into a wasp, he stung the high god's forehead. The startled god released the trapped soul, and the shaman carried it down to earth.

Animals appear in many myths, sometimes as the ancestors or mates of humans. The Yukaghir people, for example, told of an ancestral hero who was the offspring of a man who spent the

The Making of a Shaman

One Siberian myth tells of a hero who followed a golden bird up the World Tree. The bird changed into many shapes, finally becoming a woman, whom the hero wished to marry. First, however, he had to destroy an extra sun and moon that were making the world too hot and too cold. For help, the hero turned to a sea god, who boiled the hero in an iron kettle and then shaped the fragments into a new man of iron, armed with iron weapons. The hero used these to shoot the extra sun and moon. The destruction and remaking of the hero's body may symbolize the making of a shaman, during which the person is reborn with magical powers.

shaman person thought to possess spiritual and healing powers

† See *Names and Places* at the end of this volume for further information.

Shamans held a central role in Siberian religion and mythology. They were believed to travel between worlds and communicate with spirits through ceremonies and trances.

winter in the cave of a female bear. The Evenk people had stories of mammoths, immense animals that roamed the land many, many years ago. They explained how these creatures had shaped the earth by moving mud with their tusks, created rivers where they walked, and formed lakes where they had lain down.

Core Myths. Siberian mythology, which includes the beliefs and myths of a number of different peoples, has many variations on the story of creation. In one, the gods Chagan-Shukuty and Otshirvani came down from heaven to find the world covered with water. Otshirvani sat on a frog or turtle while Chagan-Shukuty dove repeatedly to the bottom, bringing up a bit of mud each time. The gods piled the mud on the back of the animal, which eventually sank into the water, leaving only the earth on the surface. In other stories Otshirvani took the form of a giant bird that fought a huge, evil serpent called Losy.

The struggle between good and evil colors Siberian mythology. The devil or chief evil spirit was named Erlik. He was sometimes said to have been a human who helped in the creation of the earth but then turned against Ulgen, the creator god. Erlik ruled the dead, and his evil spirits brought him the souls of sinners.

Siberian tradition includes myths about a great flood and a hero who saved his family. In one version, the creator god Ulgen told a man named Nama to build a boat. Into the boat Nama brought his wife, his three sons, some other people, and some animals. The boat saved them all from the flood, and they lived on the earth after it dried out. Years later Nama was close to death. His wife told him that if he killed all the animals and people he had saved in his boat, he would become king of the dead in the afterlife. Nama's son argued that the killing would be a sin, so Nama killed his wife instead and took the virtuous son to heaven, where he became a constellation of stars. ***See also*** CREATION STORIES; FLOODS; YGGDRASILL.

Sibyls

prophet one who claims to have received divine messages or insights
prophecy foretelling of what is to come; also something that is predicted

The sibyls were female **prophets** of Greek and Roman mythology. Their **prophecies,** which emerged as riddles to be interpreted by priests, were inspired by Apollo† or other gods. The number of sibyls varied from 1 to 12.

The most famous of these prophets was the Cumaean Sibyl. Apollo offered to grant her any wish if she would make love to him. Scooping up a handful of sand, the Sibyl asked to live one year for each grain of sand she held. Apollo granted her wish, but then the Sibyl refused him. As punishment, Apollo gave her long life but not

underworld land of the dead

Sigurd

Note

In German legends, Sigurd is called Siegfried; Gudrun is called Kriemhild; and Gunnar is called Gunther.

---

eternal youth. As the Sibyl grew older, she shrank in size, finally becoming so small she lived in a bottle. When someone asked the Sibyl what she wanted, she would reply that she wished only to die.

One story tells how the Cumaean Sibyl led the Greek hero Aeneas† to the **underworld** to meet his dead father Anchises. Anchises then predicted that from Aeneas would come the greatest empire the world had ever seen. According to tradition, Aeneas's descendants founded Rome.

In another well-known tale, the Sibyl offered to sell nine books to the Roman king Tarquin. He refused to buy them. The Sibyl burned three of the books and came back to offer the remaining six at the same price. Again he refused. She burned three more and returned again. This time Tarquin bought the books, which contained prophecies about the future of Rome. Tarquin kept the books in the temple of Jupiter†, where officials consulted them on special occasions to interpret the prophecies. The books were consumed in a fire in 83 B.C. ***See also*** GREEK MYTHOLOGY; ROMAN MYTHOLOGY.

In Norse† myth and legend, the warrior Sigurd was a member of the royal family of Denmark and a descendant of the god Odin†. He was raised by a blacksmith named Regin, who made him a special sword from pieces of a sword owned by Sigurd's father.

Sigurd used his sword to kill the dragon Fafnir and so acquire its golden treasure. When Sigurd roasted and ate the beast's heart, he was able to understand the language of the birds around him. They warned him that Regin was going to betray him, so Sigurd beheaded the blacksmith. Sigurd took the treasure and put a ring on his finger. He was unaware that the ring bore a curse, which brought misfortune to its wearer.

After slaying Fafnir, Sigurd came upon a castle where he awakened the warrior maiden Brunhilde, whom Odin had cast into a deep sleep. Sigurd gave his ring to Brunhilde and promised to return to marry her. But during his journey Sigurd was given a magic drink that made him forget Brunhilde, and he married the princess Gudrun instead.

Gudrun's brother Gunnar tried to win Brunhilde for himself, but Gunnar was unable to cross the wall of flames surrounding Brunhilde's castle. Sigurd, having forgotten Brunhilde completely, assumed Gunnar's shape and courted Brunhilde in his place. Believing that Sigurd had abandoned her, Brunhilde agreed to marry Gunnar, whom she did not love. When Brunhilde discovered that she had been tricked, she was both angry with Sigurd and heartbroken at the loss of his love. She had him slain and killed herself. The story of Sigurd and Brunhilde is central to Richard Wagner's series of operas known as *Der Ring des Nibelungen* (The Ring of the Nibelung). ***See also*** BRUNHILDE; NIBELUNGENLIED; NORSE MYTHOLOGY.

Sinbad the Sailor

Sinbad the Sailor appears in the *Thousand and One Nights,* a collection of Persian, Arab, and Indian tales written down between the 800s and the 1400s. A merchant from the city of Baghdad in the Near East, Sinbad made seven voyages to lands and islands around the Indian Ocean. He had great adventures, survived numerous dangers, and acquired many riches during his travels.

On Sinbad's first voyage, he and his crew visited an island that turned out to be a huge sleeping whale. When they lit a fire, the whale woke up and dived underwater. Sinbad was picked up by another ship and taken home. The second voyage took Sinbad to a desert island, where he discovered an enormous egg belonging to a giant bird called a roc. When the bird appeared, Sinbad grabbed its claw and was carried away to the Valley of Diamonds. Eventually rescued by merchants, he returned to Baghdad laden with diamonds.

During Sinbad's third voyage, the hero was captured by dwarfs and taken to the home of a one-eyed giant. The giant started eating members of his crew. Sinbad managed to escape but was lured to another island by a serpent that tried to swallow him. Once again, Sinbad got away and was rescued by a passing ship. Shipwrecked on his fourth voyage, Sinbad and his crew were taken prisoner by cannibals who planned to eat them. The hero escaped, arrived at a strange kingdom, and married the king's daughter. When she died, however, Sinbad was buried alive with her. He succeeded in getting away again.

On Sinbad's fifth voyage, his ship was destroyed by angry rocs, which dropped huge stones from the air. Washed ashore on an island, he met and killed the Old Man of the Sea. The sixth voyage saw Sinbad once again shipwrecked on an island. There he found precious stones and visited the city of Serendib, whose king sent him home with more wealth. Sinbad returned to Serendib on his final voyage. On the way home he was attacked by pirates, who sold him into slavery. While working as an elephant hunter for the merchant who bought him, Sinbad discovered an elephant burial ground and a huge store of ivory tusks. The merchant gave Sinbad his freedom and enough ivory to make him rich. His final adventure over, Sinbad returned home to Baghdad. *See also* BIRDS IN MYTHOLOGY; DWARFS AND ELVES; PERSIAN MYTHOLOGY; THOUSAND AND ONE NIGHTS.

Sirens

The Sirens were female creatures from Greek mythology whose singing lured men to destruction. Descriptions of the Sirens vary from beautiful women to monsters with the bodies of birds and human heads.

The Sirens lived on an island where they enchanted passing sailors with their song. According to some sources, sailors died when their ships crashed on the rocks near the island. Others say that sailors stayed on the island and listened to the singing until they died.

Only on two occasions did the Sirens fail to enchant passing sailors. When Jason† and the Argonauts were searching for the

epic long poem about legendary or historical heroes, written in a grand style

Golden Fleece, Orpheus† sang so sweetly that none of the crew listened to the Sirens. In Homer's† **epic** the *Odyssey,* the hero Odysseus† made his men put wax in their ears so that they could not hear the Sirens. Wanting to hear their song, Odysseus had the crew tie him to the mast so that he could not steer the ship toward the island. Some stories say the Sirens were so enraged by Odysseus that they drowned themselves in the sea. *See also* ARGONAUTS; ODYSSEY, THE; ORPHEUS.

Sisyphus

In Greek mythology, Sisyphus was famous for two things: his cleverness during life and the punishment he suffered after death. Although stories about Sisyphus differ somewhat in their details, he is usually referred to as the king of Corinth.

One story about Sisyphus involves Autolycus, a clever thief. Autolycus stole cattle by changing their color so that they could not be identified. Sisyphus outwitted him, however, by placing a mark on the cattle's hooves so that he could follow the hoofprints to the stolen animals.

nymph minor goddess of nature, usually represented as young and beautiful

In another myth, Sisyphus saw Zeus† kidnap a river **nymph,** but he promised to keep the hiding place secret. He betrayed Zeus, however, when he revealed the location to the nymph's father in exchange for a spring of pure water. Furious, Zeus sent Thanatos† (death) to take Sisyphus to Hades†. The clever Sisyphus managed to tie up Thanatos, and for days no one on earth died. Ares† went to free death and take Sisyphus to the **underworld.** Sisyphus called out to his wife not to bury him, and he persuaded Hades, ruler of the underworld, to let him go back to earth long enough to arrange a proper funeral. After returning to Corinth though, Sisyphus stayed there until his second, and final, death.

underworld land of the dead

As punishment for tricking the gods, Sisyphus was placed on a hillside in the underworld with a heavy boulder above him. To escape being crushed, he had to push the boulder uphill. The gods told him that if he rolled the stone to the other side they would release him. Each time he reached the top, though, the boulder rolled back down to the bottom, forcing Sisyphus to start over. The phrase "labor of Sisyphus" refers to any hopeless task that must be repeated endlessly. *See also* GREEK MYTHOLOGY; HADES; THANATOS.

One well-known Greek myth involves the punishment of Sisyphus, a human. After tricking the gods, Sisyphus was ordered to push a boulder uphill. But each time he reached the top of the hill, the rock rolled back to the bottom, creating endless punishment for Sisyphus.

†*See **Names and Places** at the end of this volume for further information.*

Snakes

See *Animals in Mythology; Serpents and Snakes.*

Sodom and Gomorrah

patriarch man who is the founder or oldest member of a group

According to the Old Testament of the Bible, Sodom and Gomorrah were two cities destroyed by God because of their wickedness. Apparently located near the southern end of the Dead Sea, the cities were known for the crude behavior and lack of hospitality of their inhabitants.

In the book of Genesis, the Hebrew **patriarch** Abraham begged God to spare Sodom and Gomorrah for the sake of the few good people living there. God agreed not to destroy the cities if as many as ten righteous men could be found in them. Accordingly, he sent three angels to Sodom. The angels were greeted by Lot, the only good man in either city. Lot invited the angels to his home and treated them graciously. However, that night a group of Lot's neighbors surrounded the house and demanded that he send the angels out to them. When the neighbors tried to break in, the angels told Lot to leave Sodom immediately with his family. They also warned him that no member of his family should look back at the city after leaving it.

God then sent a raging fire to consume Sodom and Gomorrah. As the cities went up in flames, Lot's wife could not resist looking back on the destruction, and God punished her by turning her into a pillar of salt. *See also* ANGELS; FIRE; SEMITIC MYTHOLOGY.

Sorcerers

See *Witches and Wizards.*

Sphinx

pharaoh ruler of ancient Egypt

The Sphinx was a legendary winged monster of Greek mythology that had the body of a lion and the head of a woman. Her siblings were Cerberus, Hydra, and the Nemean Lion. The Sphinx lived on a rock outside the city of Thebes, where she terrified the local people. Some sources say Hera† sent the Sphinx to punish the king of Thebes for carrying off one of the children of Zeus†. Others claim that Apollo† sent the monster because the Thebans failed to honor him properly.

The Sphinx posed a riddle to any passerby: "I have four legs in the morning, two legs at noon, and three legs in the evening, but I am weakest when I have the most legs. What am I?" No one was able to solve the riddle, and the Sphinx killed and devoured anyone who failed to answer correctly. Finally, the Greek hero Oedipus† provided the correct answer: "A human being walks on all fours as a baby, on two legs as an adult, and with a crutch as a third leg when he grows old." Upon hearing Oedipus's answer, the Sphinx killed herself.

Egyptian sculpture also included a type of figure called a sphinx, which had a lion's body and the head of the **pharaoh.** Egyptian sphinxes, which guarded temples and monuments, were unrelated to the Greek Sphinx. *See also* OEDIPUS.

Spider Woman

sorcerer magician or wizard

Spider Woman appears in the mythology of several Native American tribes, including the Navajo, Keresan, and Hopi. In most cases, she is associated with the emergence of life on earth. She helps humans by teaching them survival skills. Spider Woman also teaches the Navajos the art of weaving. Before weavers sit down at the loom, they often rub their hands in spider webs to absorb the wisdom and skill of Spider Woman.

In the Navajo creation story, Spider Woman (Na'ashjéii asdzáá) helps the warrior twins Monster Slayer and Child of Water find their father, the Sun. The Keresan say that Spider Woman gave the corn goddess Iyatiku a basket of seeds to plant.

According to the Hopi, at the beginning of time Spider Woman controlled the underworld, the home of the gods, while the sun god Tawa ruled the sky. Using only their thoughts, they created the earth between the two other worlds. Spider Woman molded animals from clay, but they remained lifeless. So she and Tawa spread a soft white blanket over them, said some magic words, and the creatures began to move. Spider Woman then molded people from clay. To bring them to life, she clutched them to her breast and, together with Tawa, sang a song that made them into living beings. She divided the animals and people into the groups that inhabit the earth today. She also gave men and women specific roles: Women were to watch over the home and men to pray and make offerings to the gods.

Another Hopi myth says that Tawa created insectlike beings and placed them in the First World. Dissatisfied with these creatures, Tawa sent Spider Woman to lead them, first to the Second World and then to the Third World, where they turned into people. Spider Woman taught the people how to plant, weave, and make pottery. A hummingbird gave them fire to help them warm themselves and cook their food. However, when **sorcerers** brought evil to the Third World, Spider Woman told the people to leave for the Fourth World. They planted trees to climb up to the Fourth World, but none grew tall enough. Finally, Spider Woman told them to sing to a bamboo plant so that it would grow very tall. She led the people up the bamboo stalk to the Fourth World, the one in which the Hopi currently live. ***See also*** ANIMALS IN MYTHOLOGY; CHANGING WOMAN; CORN; CREATION STORIES; NATIVE AMERICAN MYTHOLOGY.

Stars

deity god or goddess
cosmos the universe, especially as an orderly and harmonious system

Remote yet familiar, stars have fascinated people throughout history and are part of many myths and legends. Although the sun and the moon usually have the leading roles in mythology, often appearing as **deities,** the stars also appear in many stories. In some cultures, the stars represent part of the **cosmos,** such as the heavens or the home of the gods, or a path between the earth and another world. In many myths and legends, individual stars or constellations, groups of stars, have special significance.

Explaining the Stars. People who lived before electric lights and air pollution dimmed the night skies saw the heavens glittering

†See **Names and Places** at the end of this volume for further information.

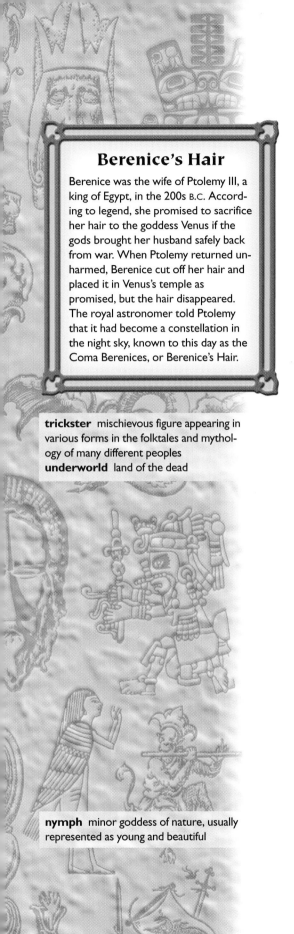

Berenice's Hair

Berenice was the wife of Ptolemy III, a king of Egypt, in the 200s B.C. According to legend, she promised to sacrifice her hair to the goddess Venus if the gods brought her husband safely back from war. When Ptolemy returned unharmed, Berenice cut off her hair and placed it in Venus's temple as promised, but the hair disappeared. The royal astronomer told Ptolemy that it had become a constellation in the night sky, known to this day as the Coma Berenices, or Berenice's Hair.

trickster mischievous figure appearing in various forms in the folktales and mythology of many different peoples
underworld land of the dead

nymph minor goddess of nature, usually represented as young and beautiful

with thousands of stars. They developed various stories to explain their brilliant presence.

The Paiute of North America describe the stars as the children of the sun and moon. Because the sun loves to eat his children, the stars disappear whenever he rises above the horizon. However, the moon, their mother, often dances happily across the sky with the stars. To the Yakut of Siberia, the stars are crystal windows that allow the gods to look down at earth. The tent-dwelling Turko-Tatar people of Central Asia picture the sky as a large tent over the earth, with the stars as tiny holes in the tent.

The Milky Way, a dense band of stars that spans the sky, marks the center of the galaxy to which our solar system belongs. In myths, however, the Milky Way has been a road, a river, and a bridge between worlds. According to a Peruvian tradition, the Vilcanota River is a reflection of the Milky Way and water constantly circulates between the two, passing from the river to heaven and back again. The Navajo say that the **trickster** Coyote created the Milky Way by tossing a blanket full of sparkling stone chips into the sky. Scattered in a great arc, the stones formed a pathway linking heaven and earth.

In many traditions, the stars have been associated with death and the afterlife. The Maya considered the Milky Way to be the road to Xibalba, the **underworld.** Many Native Americans regard the Milky Way as the path followed by the souls of the dead. According to the Zulu and Ndebele people of southern Africa, the stars are the eyes of dead ancestors, keeping watch on the living from above.

Constellations and Individual Stars in Myths. Chinese mythology includes many references to the stars. Various deities, such as the god of literature and the god of long life, were associated with the stars. One myth that occurs in several versions concerns the Weaver Girl, the goddess who weaves the clouds, and the Herdsman, who tends the cattle of heaven. The two were lovers. When the gods placed them in the sky, the Weaver Girl became the star called Vega, while the Herdsman became either the star Altair or the constellation Aquila. The gods separated the lovers with the river of the Milky Way so that they would not neglect their work. But every year, on the seventh night of the seventh month, birds formed a bridge across the Milky Way allowing the Weaver Girl and the Herdsman to meet.

People have told many tales about the group of seven stars called the Pleiades. In Greek mythology these stars were the seven daughters of the Titan Atlas† and the ocean **nymph** Pleione. According to some accounts, Zeus† placed them in the sky to protect them from the hunter Orion. But then Orion became a constellation and continued to chase the Pleiades across the heavens. The cattle-herding Masai people of Africa see the Pleiades as a group of cattle, and their appearance in the sky marks the rainy season. The Inca of South America called the Pleiades *Collca*—meaning a place where grain is stored—and believed that the constellation protected seeds and farming.

The constellation Ursa Major, called the Great Bear or the Big Dipper, appears in many Native American myths. The Seneca of New York believed that the constellation was made up of a large bear and the six hunters who chased it into the sky. The Inuit of northern Greenland, though, see Ursa Major as a giant caribou. They imagine the constellation Orion as a series of steps in the great bank of snow that connects earth and heaven.

The constellation known as the Southern Cross figures in Australian mythology. According to a story from New South Wales, it is a gum tree in which a man and a spirit are trapped, their eyes blazing forth as stars. Two other stars are white birds that rose into the sky with the tree.

Many myths and legends refer to the morning star and the evening star. These are not true stars but names for the planet Venus, which shines brightly near the horizon early or late in the night, depending on the time of year. A Norse† myth says that the morning star was originally the toe of a hero named Aurvandil. Thor† had carried Aurvandil out of Giantland and across the river Elivagar. On the way, however, one of the hero's toes froze, so Thor broke it off and threw it into the sky. To the Greeks, the evening star was Hesperus, grandfather of the goddesses called the Hesperides, who guarded the golden apples of eternal life on islands in the western sea. *See also* MOON; SUN.

Stonehenge

ritual ceremony that follows a set pattern
archaeological referring to the study of past human cultures, usually by excavating ruins

Stonehenge is a prehistoric circular monument on Salisbury Plain in southern England. It has been associated with ancient Celtic† religious **rituals** and with the Arthurian legends† of early Britain.

Constructed of ditches, earthen mounds, and immense blocks of stone, Stonehenge is now a protected **archaeological** site. Scientists have not unraveled the mysteries of its origins and purpose, but they do know that it was created in stages. Stonehenge probably began with a wooden structure sometime around 3000 B.C., and the standing stones were set in place between 2100 and 1500 B.C. Construction ended long before the time of the Celtic priests called Druids, but these religious leaders may have used Stonehenge and other ancient monuments in their rituals.

For many centuries, Stonehenge has awed and puzzled visitors. Geoffrey of Monmouth, an English historian writing in the 1100s, accounted for the monument by calling it the work of Merlin, the wizard associated with King Arthur. According to legend, Merlin used magical powers to take apart a ring of standing stones in Ireland, ship them to England, and reassemble them on

Stonehenge, a prehistoric monument in southern England, was built in several stages over thousands of years. Its precisely arranged circular design suggests that the area may have been associated with religious rituals linked to the summer solstice.

†See **Names and Places** *at the end of this volume for further information.*

Salisbury Plain. Over time the story grew more elaborate, until one version in the 1700s said that Merlin had harnessed the Devil to carry the stones to England in a single night. Other tales associated with Stonehenge explain that the stones were owned by a race of giants from Africa and had special healing powers. *See also* CELTIC MYTHOLOGY; DRUIDS; MERLIN.

Styx

underworld land of the dead

Titan one of a family of giants who ruled the earth until overthrown by the Greek gods of Olympus

In Greek mythology, Styx was one of the main rivers that ran through the **underworld.** According to legend, the boatman Charon ferried the spirits of the dead across the Styx from earth to the land of the dead.

The river was named for the eldest daughter of the **Titans** Oceanus and Tethys, who lived in a palace near the edge of the underworld. She married the Titan Pallas and had four children: Might, Force, Zeal, and Victory. Styx and her children helped Zeus† and the Olympian gods win their battle against the Titans for mastery of the universe. As a reward, Zeus ordered that an oath sworn by the waters of the Styx could never be broken, even by a god. Anyone who broke such an oath would enter a comalike state for a year and would be banished from the company of the other gods for nine more years.

The ancient Greeks identified the river Styx with a mountain stream in the land of Arcadia. They believed that its waters were poisonous and could only be held in a cup made from the hoof of a horse or a donkey. *See also* UNDERWORLD.

Sun

solar relating to the sun

deity god or goddess

pantheon all the gods of a particular culture

trickster mischievous figure appearing in various forms in the folktales and mythology of many different peoples

The largest object in the sky, the sun is the source of light, heat, and life. It can also be a symbol of destructive power. Since earliest times, people in all parts of the world have observed the position of the sun and its rising and setting throughout the year. Many cultures have created **solar** calendars to govern such things as the planting of crops and the timing of religious festivals. They have also given the sun a major place in their mythologies, often as a **deity.**

Solar Deities. The **pantheons** of many cultures have included a sun deity, usually a god but occasionally a goddess. Some myths reflect the sun's vital role in supporting life: Solar deities are often creators who bring people into existence. Native Americans from the Pacific Coast, for example, tell how the sun god Kodoyanpe and the **trickster** Coyote together created the world and set about making people to live in it.

Solar deities have also been associated with fertility of people and the earth. The Hittites of ancient Turkey worshiped Arinna, an important goddess of both the sun and fertility. In traditional myths from Uganda in Central Africa, the creator god Ruhanga, the sun god Kazooba, and the giver of life Rugaba are all the same deity.

In some mythologies, sun gods have healing powers. Shamash, the solar god of the Babylonian† people of the ancient Near East, was known as "the sun with healing in his wings." Ancient Celtic†

51

Throughout history, many different cultures had solar deities and myths about the sun. This head of the Maya sun god is located on a pyramid wall in Campeche, Mexico.

peoples had Belenus, the god of sunlight. Besides driving away the predawn mists and fogs each day, Belenus could melt away disease from the sick. When the Romans conquered the Celts, they identified Belenus with their own sun god, Apollo, who was also a god of healing.

As the most important and splendid deities of their pantheons, some solar deities have been associated with earthly rulers, the most powerful people in society. The Incas of Peru in South America regarded the sun god Inti, their chief deity, as the ancestor of the Inca royal family. According to Japanese tradition, the country's imperial family is descended from Amaterasu, the sun goddess.

Myths About the Sun. Some solar myths explain the sun's daily movement across the sky from east to west and its disappearance at night. Such stories often take the form of a journey, with the sun deity traveling across the heavens in a chariot or boat. Helios, a Greek solar deity later identified with Apollo, was a charioteer who drove his fiery vehicle through heaven by day. At night he floated back across the ocean in a golden bowl, only to mount his chariot again the next morning. The Navajo people of the American Southwest portray their sun god as a worker named Jóhonaa'éí, or sun bearer. Every day Jóhonaa'éí laboriously hauls the sun across the sky on his back. At night, he hangs the sun from a peg in the wall and rests.

The Egyptian sun god Ra made a similar circuit. Each day he traveled across the sky in his sun boat, and at night he passed through the **underworld,** greeting the dead and facing many dangers. Ra's daily cycle was more than a journey, though—it was a daily rebirth. Dawn saw the newborn sun god rise in the sky. During the morning he was a child, at noon he was mature, and by sunset he was an old man ready for death. Each sunrise was a celebration of the god's return, a victory of life over the forces of death and darkness.

The Celts also viewed the sun's journey as a cycle of death and rebirth but on a yearly rather than a daily cycle, with midwinter as death and spring as rebirth. The Celtic celebration called Beltane, held in spring, honored their sun god Belenus.

In some solar myths the sun is paired with the moon. The two may be husband and wife, brother and sister, or two brothers. In the mythology of many Native Americans, the sun god and moon god are sister and brother who also become forbidden lovers. The moon god's face is smeared with ash from the sun's fires, which accounts for the dark patches on the moon's surface. In

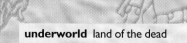

underworld land of the dead

Too Many Suns

If one sun is good, are ten suns ten times better? Not according to the Chinese myth of Yi and the ten suns. Yi, a famous soldier, was an archer of great skill. At that time, ten suns lived in the Fu Sang tree beyond the eastern edge of the world. Normally the suns took turns lighting the earth, one sun at a time. The suns grew rebellious, and one day all ten of them rose into the sky at the same time. The extra light and heat pleased the people below—until their crops shriveled and their rivers began to dry up. The Lord of Heaven sent Yi, the divine archer, to handle the problem. Yi shot nine of the suns out of the sky.

Sunjata

epic long poem about legendary or historical heroes, written in a grand style
supernatural related to forces beyond the normal world; magical or miraculous

some accounts, the moon flees in shame when he learns that his lover is also his sister. This is why the moon leaves the sky when the sun comes near.

Many cultures have myths of monsters or evil spirits that steal or devour the sun or stories of the sun falling from the heavens or withdrawing its light for a time. Some of these myths may explain eclipses, times when the earth's shadow temporarily blots out the sun or moon. A solar eclipse creates a period of eerie near-darkness in the middle of the day—an event that surely cried out for a reassuring explanation.

A well-known myth about the Japanese sun goddess Amaterasu tells how she became so angry with her brother, who was misbehaving, that she retreated into a cave. The goddess's withdrawal deprived the world of light and warmth. Finally, the other gods tricked her into emerging.

According to a traditional myth from the Hindu Kush mountains of Afghanistan, the giant Espereg-era once stole the sun and the moon. The hero god Mandi disguised himself as a child and tricked the giants into adopting him. After a time with the giants, Mandi rescued the sun and moon and rode off with them on a magical horse. The supreme god then hurled them into the sky to shine on the world. ***See also*** **AMATERASU; APOLLO; ATEN; INTI; LUG; MITHRAS; MOON; RA (RE); SHAMASH; STARS.**

Sunjata is the hero of an African **epic** of people living in the southern Sahara. He may be based on a king named Sundiata or Sundjata, who founded the kingdom of Mali around A.D. 1240. His story is filled with **supernatural** elements, from the hero's mysterious birth to his extraordinary strength.

The epic of Sunjata begins with the hero's childhood. The son of the king of Manding, Sunjata was born under unusual circumstances. His mother was pregnant with him for eight years, when a magical spirit called a jinni (or genie) told Sunjata's father that the boy would someday become a great king.

As a child, Sunjata performed many amazing deeds and earned the name Mari Djata (the Lion of Manding) because he could transform himself into a lion. Sunjata's father grew afraid of him and used his power to paralyze the boy. But after seven years, the king recognized Sunjata's wisdom and restored his son to health. Sunjata's miraculous deeds continued. He taught wild animals to gather firewood and helped a group of witches bring back to life a boy whom they had killed.

Sunjata lived in the countryside, killing 800 elephants and 8,000 lions. However, on the death of his father, he returned to Manding and won a competition with one of his brothers to become king. The young ruler's first task was to kill a terrible beast, a witch in the shape of an animal, that had been terrorizing the people. The old witch was so impressed by Sunjata's kindness and wisdom that she told him how to kill her. He did so and became a hero. Later, Sunjata went to war against a wicked king who

claimed his throne. After defeating this demon king, with the help of his sister, Sunjata went on to conquer an extensive area that became the empire of Mali. According to legend, Sunjata ruled with fairness and in peace. *See also* AFRICAN MYTHOLOGY; HEROES; WITCHES AND WIZARDS.

Susano-ô

deity god or goddess

A complex Japanese god, Susano-ô was associated with storms and the sea in mythology. His connection with water began at birth. He was formed from drops of water that were shed when the creator god Izanagi washed his nose. Susano-ô sometimes caused trouble for the other **deities,** including his sister, the sun goddess Amaterasu, and brother, the moon god Tsuki-yomi.

Although placed in charge of the sea, Susano-ô envied his sister's power over the sun and his brother's control of the moon. Susano-ô behaved so badly while visiting Amaterasu's court that she hid in a cave, taking the sunlight with her. The other gods eventually lured the sun goddess out of the cave. Then they punished Susano-ô by cutting off his beard, fingernails, and toenails and expelling him from heaven.

Susano-ô went to live in Izumo in western Japan, where he had various adventures and began to use his powers for good. According to one story, he met an old man and woman who were grieving because seven of their daughters had been eaten by an eight-headed serpent. Susano-ô killed the monster by getting it drunk and cutting off its heads. In gratitude, the old couple gave Susano-ô their remaining daughter in marriage. Other stories say that Susano-ô took water from the sea and brought it to the land as rain. He also made forests by cutting his beard and hair and planting the strands on mountainsides. *See also* AMATERASU; IZANAGI AND IZANAMI; JAPANESE MYTHOLOGY; KOJIKI; NIHONGI; SERPENTS AND SNAKES.

Ta'aroa

The creator god Ta'aroa appears in many myths from Polynesia, the vast region that includes hundreds of islands in the Pacific Ocean. In some parts of Polynesia, Ta'aroa is known by different names. In addition to his role as creator, he is often associated with the sea.

To the people of Tahiti, Ta'aroa is the supreme god of creation. Before the world was made, he lived inside a shell called Rumia (upset), until he tipped his shell and fell out into a dark void. He created a new shell and waited for ages before coming out again. Then he formed the earth from one of the shells and the sky from the other. He created the other deities as well as plants, animals, and people to fill the world. According to some versions of the story, Ta'aroa made the earth from his own body, forming soil from his flesh, mountains from his bones, and living things from his blood. Everything in the world came from Ta'aroa.

The people of Samoa call the god Tangaloa and say that he created the islands of Samoa by throwing down rocks from heaven.

† See *Names and Places* at the end of this volume for further information.

The Maori of New Zealand call him Tangaroa, one of the children of the sky god and the earth goddess. The creator of the islands, Tangaroa is also the god of the ocean and its creatures. ***See also*** **CREATION STORIES; POLYNESIAN MYTHOLOGY; RANGI AND PAPA.**

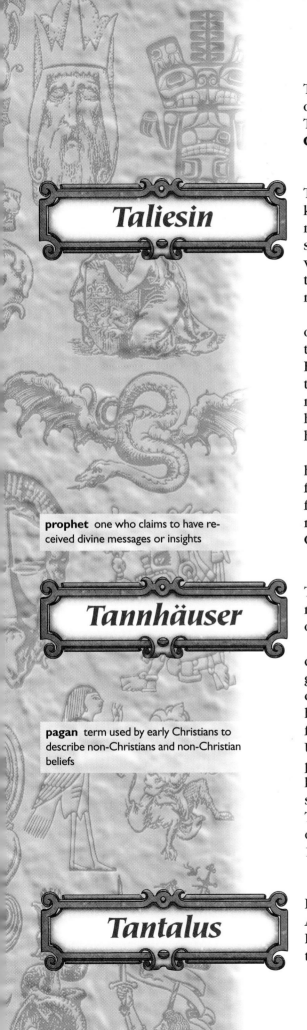

Taliesin

Taliesin was a Welsh poet of the A.D. 500s who inspired a well-known legend of Celtic† mythology. It happened that a witch named Caridwen had a very ugly son. To make up for his looks, she decided to prepare a magic potion that would give him all the world's knowledge. However, the pot containing the potion had to boil for a year, so she asked Taliesin—then a poor farm boy named Gwion—to watch the pot for her.

One day the pot bubbled over, and a drop of the liquid splashed on Gwion's finger. When he licked his finger, he received one-third of the world's knowledge and the ability to change his form. He also realized that Caridwen was going to kill him when the potion was ready, so he ran away. He assumed the shape of many animals but could not get away from Caridwen. Finally, he turned himself into a grain of wheat, and Caridwen—in the form of a hen—ate him.

Nine months later, Caridwen gave birth to Gwion. She sewed him into a leather bag and tossed it into a river. A Welsh prince found the bag, and when he opened it he saw the boy's shining face. He named the child Taliesin (meaning shining brow) and raised him in the royal court, where he became one of the greatest Celtic **prophets** and poets. ***See also*** **WITCHES AND WIZARDS.**

prophet one who claims to have received divine messages or insights

Tannhäuser

Tannhäuser was the name of a wandering poet who lived in Germany during the A.D. 1200s. This historical figure became the subject of a famous legend.

According to the story, Tannhäuser one day came across an underground cave that happened to be the home of Venus, the Roman goddess of love. He remained with Venus for a year but eventually came to yearn for the life he left behind. When Venus agreed to let him return to the world, he went to Rome to ask Pope Urban IV to forgive him for making love to the **pagan** goddess. However, Urban said that Tannhäuser could no more be forgiven than the pope's wooden staff could produce fresh flowers. Three days later, the staff began to blossom, and Urban, realizing his mistake, sent messengers to find Tannhäuser. However, denied forgiveness, Tannhäuser had already returned to Venus's cave to spend the rest of his days with her. Richard Wagner's opera *Tannhäuser* from 1845 is based on this story.

pagan term used by early Christians to describe non-Christians and non-Christian beliefs

Tantalus

In Greek mythology, Tantalus, king of Lydia, was the son of Zeus†. A favorite of the gods, he was often invited to dine at their feasts. But Tantalus angered the gods. Some stories say that he betrayed their secrets to mortals, while others claim that he stole the food

underworld land of the dead

deity god or goddess

of the gods. Another myth gives a more gruesome explanation, saying that Tantalus killed his son Pelops and served the flesh to the gods to prove they could not tell the difference between human and animal meat.

To punish Tantalus, the gods placed him in a pool of water in the **underworld** that was surrounded by fruit trees. When he went to drink, the water would recede. When he tried to eat the fruit, it moved out of reach. Tantalus's punishment gave rise to the word *tantalizing,* meaning something that is tempting but just out of reach.

Telepinu

Telepinu was the god of agriculture of the Hittites, people who lived in the ancient Near East in what is now Syria and Turkey. Like his father the storm god, Telepinu had a quick temper. When he was angry, plants and animals ceased to grow and people suffered.

According to a Hittite legend, Telepinu awoke one day in such a terrible mood that he put his boots on the wrong feet. Enraged, he stormed off into the countryside. After a while he became tired and lay down in a meadow to sleep.

While Telepinu was away, the earth dried up completely. All the plants and trees died for lack of water. Animals and humans stopped giving birth. The land was barren and nearly lifeless. Alarmed, the sun god sent an eagle to find Telepinu, but the eagle could not locate him. Then the great mother goddess Hannahanna asked the storm god to find his son, but he too failed.

Finally Hannahanna sent a bee to seek the missing god. The other **deities** thought the plan was crazy. If they could not locate Telepinu, how could a mere bee do so? But the bee searched in places the gods did not think to look and eventually found Telepinu asleep in the meadow. Following Hannahanna's instructions, the bee stung Telepinu several times. Although the stings woke the god, they only made him angrier. So the sun god sent Kamrusepas, the goddess of healing, to soothe Telepinu's temper. When Telepinu returned to his temple, the plants and animals resumed their growth, and the people thrived again. ***See also*** Semitic Mythology.

Tell, William

William Tell, a hero of Swiss folklore, became a symbol of Switzerland's national pride and independence. He is best known for shooting an arrow through an apple sitting on his son's head.

Tell's feat of archery supposedly took place around 1300, when Switzerland was under Austrian rule. The independent-minded Tell refused to salute an Austrian official, who then ordered Tell to take the nerve-wracking shot. Afterward, the official spotted a second arrow. Tell said that if his first arrow had missed, he would have used the second one to kill the official. As punishment, Tell was sent to prison, but he escaped and killed the Austrian official. This act inspired the rebellion that eventually ended Austrian rule in Switzerland. Some accounts name Tell a leader in that fight.

† *See **Names and Places** at the end of this volume for further information.*

William Tell is a Swiss hero and a symbol of independence. In this illustration, an actor plays the role of William Tell in Rossini's opera.

William Tell first appeared in legends and songs of the 1400s. By the 1700s, various Swiss histories featured the story. The play *Wilhelm Tell* (1804) by the German poet Friedrich von Schiller brought the Swiss hero to world attention, as did the opera *Guillaume Tell* (1829) by Italian composer Gioacchino Rossini. Despite these works, however, there is no historical evidence that William Tell existed, although the stories about him may have been based on a kernel of reality. The famous test of marksmanship, with a cherished life at stake, is similar to stories from Norse† and British folklore.

Tezcatlipoca

divination act or practice of foretelling the future
deity god or goddess
patron special guardian, supporter, or protector

Tezcatlipoca was one of the most important gods of the Aztecs of central Mexico. His name, meaning Lord of the Smoking Mirror, refers to the mirrors made of obsidian, a shiny black stone, that Aztec priests used in **divination.**

Tezcatlipoca played many contradictory roles in Aztec mythology. Like other Aztec **deities,** he could be both helpful and destructive. As a god of the sun, he ripened the crops but could also send a burning drought that killed the plants. The **patron** god of helpless folk such as orphans and slaves, he was also the patron of

trickster mischievous figure appearing in various forms in the folktales and mythology of many different peoples

underworld land of the dead

oracle priest or priestess or other creature through whom a god is believed to speak; also the location (such as a shrine) where such words are spoken

royalty, and he gloried in war and human sacrifice. Another of Tezcatlipoca's roles was to punish sinners and cheats, but he himself could not be trusted.

Although associated with the sun, Tezcatlipoca was even more strongly linked with night and its dark mysteries, including dreams, sorcery, witches, and demons. Legend said that he roamed the earth each night in the form of a skeleton whose ribs opened like doors. If a person met Tezcatlipoca and was bold enough to reach through those doors and seize his heart, the god would promise riches and power in order to be released. He would not keep his promises, though.

As a **trickster** god, Tezcatlipoca delighted in overturning the order of things, causing conflict and confusion. Sometimes, these disruptions could also be a source of creative energy and positive change. Tezcatlipoca's ultimate trick was one he played on his fellow god Quetzalcoatl. After introducing Quetzalcoatl to drunkenness and other vices, he used his mirror to show Quetzalcoatl how weak and degraded he had become. Quetzalcoatl fled the world in shame, leaving it to Tezcatlipoca. He did, however, promise to return at the end of a 52-year cycle. *See also* AZTEC MYTHOLOGY; QUETZALCOATL.

Thanatos

In Greek mythology, Thanatos was the symbol of death. When humans died, he cut off a lock of their hair and took them to the **underworld.** Thanatos was the son of Nyx (night) and the brother of Hypnos (sleep).

In one famous myth, a woman named Alcestis agreed to let Thanatos take her in the place of her husband, Admetus. However, when Thanatos appeared before her, the hero Hercules† wrestled him and forced him to release Alcestis. A different story tells how a mortal named Sisyphus tricked Thanatos. As a punishment, Sisyphus was forced to spend eternity rolling a boulder up a hill in the underworld. As soon as it reached the top, it would roll to the bottom again. *See also* ALCESTIS; SISYPHUS.

Theseus

Theseus, a hero of Greek mythology, is best known for slaying a monster called the Minotaur. His life and adventures illustrate many themes of Greek myths, including the idea that even the mightiest hero cannot escape tragedy, if that is his fate.

Mysterious Origins. Like many other heroes of myth and legend, Theseus was born and raised in unusual and dramatic circumstances. His mother was Aethra, daughter of King Pittheus of Troezen. Although some accounts name Poseidon† as his father, most say that Theseus was the son of King Aegeus of Athens, who had stopped at Troezen after consulting the **oracle** at Delphi.

The oracle had warned Aegeus not to get drunk or father a child on his way home to Athens—or one day he would die of sorrow. However, at Troezen, Aegeus ignored the warnings and became

Related Entries
Other entries related to Theseus are listed at the end of this article.

Aethra's lover. Before leaving for Athens, he placed his sandals and sword under a boulder and told Aethra that if she bore a son who could lift the boulder, that son would inherit the throne of Athens.

Theseus grew into a strong young man, and one day he easily lifted the boulder and retrieved the sandals and the sword. He then set off for Athens to claim his heritage. On the way, he faced a series of challenges: three vicious and murderous outlaws; a monstrous pig that was destroying the countryside; a king who challenged travelers to fatal wrestling matches; and an innkeeper named Procrustes who tortured people by either stretching them or chopping off their limbs to make them fit his beds. Theseus overcame these dangerous opponents and killed them by the same methods they had used against their victims.

Meeting the Minotaur. Upon arriving in Athens, Theseus found King Aegeus married to an enchantress named Medea. Medea tried to poison Theseus. But when Aegeus saw the young man's sword and sandals, he realized that Theseus was his son and saved him from the poison. Medea fled, and Theseus became heir to the Athenian throne. He continued his heroic feats, defeating a plot against his father and destroying a savage wild bull.

Theseus, a hero of Greek mythology, is best known for slaying a monster called the Minotaur. When Theseus entered the Labyrinth where the Minotaur lived, he took a ball of yarn to unwind and mark his route. Once he found the Minotaur and killed it, Theseus used the string to find his way out of the maze.

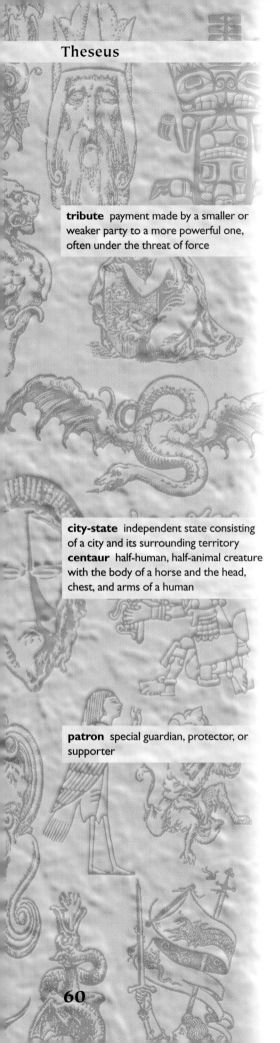

tribute payment made by a smaller or weaker party to a more powerful one, often under the threat of force

city-state independent state consisting of a city and its surrounding territory
centaur half-human, half-animal creature with the body of a horse and the head, chest, and arms of a human

patron special guardian, protector, or supporter

Athens labored under a terrible curse. Earlier Aegeus had sent another warrior, the son of King Minos of Crete, against the bull. The prince had died, and in revenge King Minos called down a plague on the Athenians. Only by sending seven young men and seven young women to Crete every year could they obtain relief. In Crete the youths were sacrificed to the Minotaur, a monstrous man-bull that lived below Minos's castle in a maze called the Labyrinth.

Determined to end this grim **tribute,** Theseus volunteered to be one of the victims. When the Athenians reached Crete, Minos's daughter Ariadne fell in love with Theseus. (Some accounts say that Aphrodite†, whose help Theseus had requested, filled the girl's heart with passion.) Before Theseus entered the Labyrinth, Ariadne gave him a ball of yarn and told him to unwind it on his way in so that he could find his way out again. Deep in the maze Theseus met the Minotaur and killed it with a blow from his fist. He and the other Athenians then set sail for Athens, taking Ariadne with them. Along the way, they stopped at the island of Naxos, where Theseus abandoned Ariadne.

Theseus had promised his father that if he returned safely to Athens he would raise a white sail on his homecoming ship. He forgot to do so, however, and left the black sail hoisted. When Aegeus saw the black-sailed vessel approaching, he killed himself in grief, thus fulfilling the prophecy he had heard at Delphi.

Later Adventures. On his father's death, Theseus became king of the **city-state** of Athens, where he won honor and was credited with enlarging the kingdom. His name sometimes appears in myths about heroic deeds, such as a battle against the **centaurs** or the quest of Jason and the Argonauts for the Golden Fleece†. Theseus also went to war against the female warriors known as Amazons, and he captured and married one of them—either Hippolyta, the Amazon queen, or her sister Antiope. This wife bore him a son, Hippolytus.

After his Amazon wife died, Theseus eventually married Phaedra, said to be a sister of Ariadne. Phaedra fell passionately in love with her stepson, Hippolytus, who rejected her love. The scorned Phaedra hanged herself, leaving a letter in which she accused Hippolytus of raping her. Furious, Theseus asked his **patron** Poseidon to destroy Hippolytus, and the god fulfilled the king's wish. Later, Theseus learned the truth and knew that he had wrongly had his only son killed.

Theseus's final adventures were less than glorious. Seeking another wife, he kidnapped a daughter of Zeus† (Helen of Sparta, later known as Helen of Troy). He also became involved in a plot to carry off Persephone, queen of the underworld. These events brought trouble upon Athens, and the people drove Theseus away. Now a lonely old man, Theseus took refuge on the island of Skyros, but the local king, regarding Theseus as a possible rival, pushed the hero off a cliff to his death. ***See also*** **AMAZONS; ARGONAUTS; ARIADNE; DELPHI; GREEK MYTHOLOGY; HEROES; MEDEA; MINOS; MINOTAUR; PHAEDRA; PROCRUSTES.**

† See **Names and Places** *at the end of this volume for further information.*

Thetis

nymph minor goddess of nature, usually represented as young and beautiful

immortal able to live forever

According to Greek mythology, Thetis was a sea **nymph** who gave birth to the famous hero Achilles†. The gods Zeus† and Neptune† both desired Thetis, but they did not pursue her because it was foretold that the son she bore would become greater than his father. So the gods arranged for Thetis to marry Peleus, a mortal.

The nymph did not wish to marry Peleus, however, and she changed into a sea monster and many other shapes to escape. Peleus held her until she changed back into a woman and agreed to marry him. Thetis bore him six sons, and she tried to make each son **immortal** by burning the child in a fire. She failed each time but tried again when she gave birth to a seventh son, Achilles. When Peleus discovered Thetis holding Achilles in the fire, he became so angry with her that she left him.

In a later version of the myth, Thetis dipped Achilles into the river Styx to make him immortal, but she forgot to wet the heel by which she held him. Achilles was later killed during the Trojan War† when the warrior Paris shot an arrow into his unprotected heel. *See also* ACHILLES; PELEUS; STYX.

Thor

deity god or goddess
patron special guardian, protector, or supporter

Thor was the god of thunder and of the sky in Norse† and early Germanic mythology. Though Odin† held a higher rank, Thor seems to have been the best loved and most worshiped of the Norse **deities.** He belonged to the common people, while Odin appealed to the learned and noble classes. A **patron** of farmers, Thor was associated with weather and crops. Although he could be fearsome, many myths portray him in a comic and affectionate way.

Origins and Qualities. Thor appears throughout Norse mythology as a huge, strongly built, red-bearded fellow with a huge appetite. He grew out of Donar or Thunor, an ancient god of sky and thunder. Some myths say that Thor was the son of Odin and Fjorgyn, the earth goddess. His wife was the beautiful goddess Sif, who seldom appears in myths and remains a somewhat mysterious figure.

Generally good-natured, Thor had a hot temper, and his anger was dreadful to behold. He was a fierce enemy of the frost giants, the foes of the Norse gods. When people heard thunder and saw lightning in the sky, they knew that Thor was fighting these evil giants.

The thunder god's chief weapon was his mighty hammer Mjollnir, or Crusher, which the dwarfs had forged for him. When he threw Mjollnir, it returned magically to his hand like a boomerang. Among Mjollnir's other powers was the gift of restoring life to the dead. The connection of Thor's hammer with life and fertility gave rise to the old Norse customs of placing a hammer in a bride's lap at her wedding and of raising it over a newborn child.

Thor's treasures also included a magical belt that doubled his strength whenever he wore it and a pair of goats, Tanngniost and Tanngrisni (both "Toothgnashers"), that pulled his chariot across the sky. Whenever he was overcome with hunger, Thor would devour his goats, only to return them to life with Mjollnir.

Thor, the Norse god of thunder and the sky, appears in the center of this tapestry holding his mighty hammer.

trickster mischievous figure appearing in various forms in the folktales and mythology of many different peoples

Myths About Thor. According to one well-known myth about Thor, Thrym, king of the giants, came into possession of Mjollnir and declared that he would give it back to Thor only if the beautiful goddess Freyja agreed to marry him. She angrily refused, and the **trickster** god Loki came up with a clever plan to recover Mjollnir. Using women's clothing and a bridal veil to disguise Thor as Freyja, Loki escorted "Freyja" to Jotunheim, the home of the giants. Thrym greeted his bride, though he was surprised at her appetite at the wedding feast. "Freyja" consumed an entire ox, three barrels of wine, and much more. Loki explained that she had been unable to eat for a week because of her excitement at marrying Thrym. The giant accepted this explanation, and the wedding proceeded. When the time came for a hammer to be placed in the bride's lap according to custom, Thor grabbed Mjollnir and threw off his disguise. Then he used the hammer to smash the giants and their hall.

During another visit to Jotunheim, Thor and Loki met Skrymir, an especially large giant. He was so big that when they wandered into one of his gloves, they thought they were in a mansion and slept in one of the fingers. In the morning they found Skrymir sleeping, and Thor tried to crush the giant's head with Mjollnir. Skrymir simply brushed away the blow as though it were no more than a falling leaf.

The gods traveled on to Utgard, a city of giants, where the giants challenged Thor to drain their drinking cup and lift their cat from the floor. He could not do either—the cup was connected to the sea, and the cat was really Jormungand, the serpent that encircles the world. Although Thor failed the tests, he came close to draining the ocean and removing the world serpent.

Several early Norse sources recount the myth of Thor's encounter with the giant Hymir. Thor disguised himself as a young man and went fishing with Hymir, first killing the giant's largest ox to use for bait. Thor then rowed their boat far out of sight of land and cast his hook. Something bit at the ox, and Thor drew up his line to discover that he had hooked Jormungand, the giant serpent. Placing his feet on the ocean floor, Thor pulled and pulled on the line, while the serpent spit out poison. Just as Thor was about to strike Jormungand with his hammer, Hymir cut the line and the serpent sank back down to the depths. Many myths say, however, that Thor and Jormungand remained bitter enemies, fated to fight again on the day called Ragnarok, the end of the world, when they will kill one another. ***See also*** LOKI; NORSE MYTHOLOGY; ODIN.

Thoth

patron special guardian, protector, or supporter
scribe secretary or writer

underworld land of the dead

Thoth was the Egyptian god of wisdom and knowledge. Honored as the inventor of writing and the founder of branches of learning such as art, astronomy, medicine, law, and magic, he was the **patron** god of **scribes.** Ancient Egyptians associated Thoth with the moon and identified him as the son—or heart and tongue—of Ra, the supreme sun god.

According to legend, Thoth possessed books of wisdom that contained secret information about nature and magic. Although the books were hidden, certain scribes had access to them.

Thoth played a key role in the Egyptian story of the afterlife. Known to be fair and impartial, Thoth judged the souls of the dead by weighing their hearts against a feather that represented truth. After recording the results, he told Osiris, ruler of the **underworld,** whether the individual had led a just life. In works of art, Thoth appears as either a human with the head of an ibis— a bird with a long, curved bill—or a baboon that supports the moon on its head. *See also* AFTERLIFE; EGYPTIAN MYTHOLOGY; MOON; OSIRIS; RA (RE); UNDERWORLD.

Thousand and One Nights

Thousand and One Nights, also called *The Arabian Nights' Entertainment* or simply *The Arabian Nights,* is a sprawling, centuries-old collection of tales. In the English-speaking world, it is the best-known work of Arabic stories.

The framework of the collection is that a king named Shahriyar, distrustful of women, had the habit of taking a new wife every night and killing her the next day. A resourceful young woman named Shahrazad had a plan to end the deadly tradition. After

Thousand and One Nights, also known as *The Arabian Nights,* is a collection of Arabic tales, fables, and poems.

marrying the king, she told him a story on their wedding night with the promise to finish it the next day. He let her live, and she repeated the trick. So captivating were her stories that Shahriyar spared her life again and again in order to hear the rest of the narrative.

The origins of *Thousand and One Nights* are unknown. The oldest bit of Arabic text dates from the 800s; the first lengthy text was written in the 1400s. None of the early Arabic-language texts contains exactly the same stories. Scholars have identified Persian, Baghdadian, and Egyptian elements in the work, which seems to have developed over the years as an ever-changing collection of fairy tales, romances, fables, poems, legends about heroes, and humorous stories. The stories that are best known in the English-speaking world—those of Sinbad the Sailor, Aladdin and his Magic Lamp, and Ali Baba and the Forty Thieves—do not appear in all editions of *Thousand and One Nights*. *See also* ALADDIN; SINBAD THE SAILOR.

Thunderbird

An important figure in Native American mythology, the Thunderbird represents the natural forces of thunder, lightning, and storms. It is also believed to protect humans by fighting evil spirits. Many groups have their own stories about the bird.

The Thunderbird is one of the main gods of the sky. It creates thunder by flapping its wings and causes lightning by opening and closing its beak and eyes. Usually described as a huge bird, the Thunderbird is large enough to carry off a whale to eat and to split open trees to find insects for food.

The Algonquian people consider Thunderbirds to be ancestors of the human race, involved with the creation of the universe. According to a Shawnee tale, Thunderbirds appear as boys and can speak backwards. Other cultures believe in four Thunderbirds that guard a nest holding an egg, which hatches all other birds of their type.

A Lakota Sioux myth says that the great Thunderbird Wakan Tanka was the grandson of the sky spirit that created the world and put people on it. But the water spirit Unktehi thought the people were lice, and she and her followers tried to drown them. The people retreated to the highest hill they could find and prayed for help. Wakan Tanka came to fight Unktehi and sent lightning crashing to earth. The ground split open, and Unktehi and her followers drained into the cracks. As a result, humankind was saved. *See also* BIRDS IN MYTHOLOGY; NATIVE AMERICAN MYTHOLOGY; WAKAN TANKA.

Tiamat

In the Babylonian creation story called the *Enuma Elish,* Tiamat was a **primeval** goddess of salt waters and **chaos.** At the beginning of the universe, she and Apsu, the spirit of fresh waters, gave birth to all the gods. Tiamat's son Ea soon challenged and killed Apsu, but he could not defeat Tiamat. Ea then enlisted the help of

his son Marduk, who rode out in a chariot to do battle with Tiamat in the form of a dragon. As Marduk approached, Tiamat opened her mouth to swallow him. But Marduk threw a storm into Tiamat's mouth, which prevented her from closing it. Then he killed her by shooting an arrow into her belly. After cutting Tiamat's body into pieces, Marduk used them to create the heavens and the earth. *See also* CREATION STORIES; ENUMA ELISH; MARDUK; SEMITIC MYTHOLOGY.

Tiki

In the mythology of some Polynesian peoples, Tiki was the first man on earth. There are several versions of Tiki's story. According to the Maori, the god Tumatauenga created Tiki. One day Tiki saw a woman swimming in a lake and was overcome by her beauty. The woman seduced Tiki and the two eventually married.

In another tale, Tiki saw his own reflection in a pool of water. Thinking it was a person, he dove into the water, causing the image to vanish. Later Tiki saw his reflection in another pool, but this time he covered the water with dirt so that the image could not escape. The dirt developed into a woman. One day when the woman was bathing, an eel entered the water and the woman experienced a feeling of desire. She then seduced Tiki. *See also* POLYNESIAN MYTHOLOGY.

Tiresias

Tiresias, a blind **prophet,** appears in many Greek myths. Several tales account for his blindness. One tells that he was struck blind as a boy when he saw Athena† bathing. Later Athena felt sorry for Tiresias but could not restore his sight. Instead, she gave him the gift of **prophecy** and the ability to understand the language of the birds.

In another myth, Tiresias came across two snakes mating. He killed the female snake and was transformed into a woman. Seven years later, he again saw two mating snakes; this time he killed the male snake and became a man. Because he had been both man and woman, Zeus† and Hera† asked him to settle an argument: Which of the sexes enjoys love more? When Tiresias replied that man gives more pleasure than he receives, Hera struck him blind. To make up for this deed, Zeus gave Tiresias the ability to foresee the future and allowed him to live an extraordinarily long life.

One of Tiresias's gifts was that his spirit could still utter prophecies in the **underworld.** In the *Odyssey†*, the hero Odysseus goes to the underworld to seek advice from Tiresias. In the story of Oedipus†, Tiresias revealed that Oedipus had killed his father and married his own mother. In *Antigone* by Sophocles, Tiresias warns Creon against punishing Antigone for burying her brother. In yet another tale, Tiresias warned Pentheus, the king of Thebes, to pay tribute to the god Dionysus†. Pentheus, however, refused to listen to Tiresias and was torn to pieces by a group of Dionysus's followers called the Maenads. *See also* SEERS.

Titans

primeval from the earliest times

underworld land of the dead

The Titans were gigantic, powerful, and **primeval** beings that loomed in the background of many Greek myths and tales. Children of Uranus (the sky) and Gaia (the earth), the Titans ruled the world before they were overthrown by the god Zeus† and his five brothers and sisters.

The Greek writer Hesiod† listed six male Titans—Oceanus, Coeus, Cronus, Crius, Hyperion, and Iapetus—and six female Titanesses—Tethys, Themis, Phoebe, Mnemosyne, Theia, and Rhea. Some accounts add the brothers Prometheus†, Epimetheus, and Atlas† and the moon goddess Selene to this group of Titans. These four gods and a few others, however, are more often described as children of the original 12 Titans.

Zeus and his siblings, the first of the Olympian gods, were the children of Cronus and Rhea. Their battle to overthrow the Titans and take possession of the universe is the backdrop of Greek mythology. The Olympian gods eventually won, and Zeus is said to have thrown those who stood against him into Tartarus, a deep pit in the **underworld.**

The Titans represent huge, primitive, and hard-to-control forces. They also symbolize a spirit of rebellion against the authority of the gods, as in the story of the Titan Prometheus, who helped human beings against Zeus's will. The immense size of the Titans is the source of the modern word *titanic,* meaning extremely large. ***See also*** ATLAS; CRONUS; GAIA; GREEK MYTHOLOGY; PROMETHEUS; URANUS; ZEUS.

Tlaloc

Mesoamerica cultural region consisting of southern Mexico and northern regions of Central America

To the Aztecs of central Mexico, Tlaloc was a god of rain and fertility. Associated with lightning, thunder, and vegetation, he appeared as a man with circles around his eyes and fangs like the teeth of a jaguar. Tlaloc shared the main temple in the Aztec capital of Tenochtitlán with the gods Quetzalcoatl and Huitzilopochtli. The Maya of **Mesoamerica** called Tlaloc Chac, and the Quiché of Guatemala knew him as Tohil.

Tlaloc had both helpful and harmful aspects. He carried four water jugs: one gave rain, but the others poured disease, frost, and drought onto the world. He and his wife, Chalchiuhtlicue, supervised the Tlaloque, spirits in charge of weather and mountains. The Tlaloque delivered rain to the earth and produced thunder by clashing their water jugs together.

Like other Aztec deities, Tlaloc required human sacrifice. Priests sacrificed children to him during the dry season. According to tradition, if the victims cried during the proceedings, their tears were a sign of plentiful rain to come.

One level of the Aztec heavens was named Tlalocan after the god. It was a place of abundant vegetation and everlasting spring. The souls of the dead who were sacred to Tlaloc—victims of drowning, lightning, and certain diseases such as leprosy—went to this lush garden paradise. ***See also*** AZTEC MYTHOLOGY; HUITZILOPOCHLI; MAYAN MYTHOLOGY; QUETZALCOATL.

†*See **Names and Places** at the end of this volume for further information.*

Trees in Mythology

supernatural related to forces beyond the normal world; magical or miraculous

underworld land of the dead
cosmic large or universal in scale; having to do with the universe
immortality ability to live forever

Forests play a prominent role in many folktales and legends. In these dark, mysterious places, heroes can lose their way, face unexpected challenges, and stumble on hidden secrets. Part of the age-old magic of forests lies in the ideas that people have had about trees. In myths and legends from around the world, trees appear as ladders between worlds, as sources of life and wisdom, and as the physical forms of supernatural beings.

World Trees

With its roots buried deep in the earth, its trunk above ground, and its branches stretching toward the sky, a tree serves as a symbolic, living link between this world and those of supernatural beings. In many myths, a tree is a vital part of the structure of the universe. Gods and their messengers travel from world to world by climbing up or down the tree. The Norse† believed that a tree runs like an axis, or pole, through this world and the realms above and below it. They called their World Tree Yggdrasill. It was a great ash tree that nourished gods, humans, and animals, connecting all living things and all phases of existence.

In traditional societies of Latvia, Lithuania, and northern Germany, the world tree was thought to be a distant oak, birch, or apple tree with iron roots, copper branches, and silver leaves. The spirits of the dead lived in this tree. Greek folktales tell of goblins in the underworld who try to cut the roots of the tree that is holding up the earth and the sky. Norse legends contain a similar image with an evil serpent forever gnawing at Yggdrasill's roots.

The mythology of early India, preserved in texts called the *Upanishads,* includes a cosmic tree called Asvattha. It is the living universe, an aspect of Brahman, the world spirit. This cosmic tree reverses the usual order. Its roots are in the sky, and its branches grow downward to cover the earth.

Trees of Life and Knowledge

Providers of shade and bearers of fruit, trees have long been associated with life and fertility. Evergreen trees, which remain green all year, became symbols of undying life. Deciduous trees, which lose their leaves in the winter and produce new ones in the spring, symbolized renewal, rebirth after death, or immortality.

In Norse mythology, the World Tree called Yggdrasill runs like a pole through this world and the realms above and below it. Yggdrasill is a great ash tree that connects all living things and all phases of existence.

The Talking Tree

After European missionaries introduced Christianity to the Native Americans, the Yaqui of the American Southwest created a myth about a talking tree that spread the news of the new faith. One day the people came upon a tree whose vibrations made a sound that no one could understand. A wise woman who lived deep in the forest sent her daughter to interpret the sounds. The talking tree told of the Christian God and the priests who would soon arrive to teach the people new beliefs and new ways. Not everyone welcomed the coming changes. Some people left to dwell under the ground, taking the old ways with them. Those who remained became the Yaqui.

Many creation myths draw on trees as symbols of life. In some versions of the Persian† creation story, a huge tree grew from the rotting corpse of the first human. The trunk separated into a man and a woman, Mashya and Mashyane, and the fruit of the tree became the various races of humankind. Norse† mythology says that the first man and woman were an ash and an elm tree given life by the gods. The same theme appears in myths of the Algonquian-speaking people of North America, which tell that the creator and culture hero Gluskap fashioned man from an ash tree.

The tree of life, with sacred animals feeding on fruit-bearing branches, is a common image in the art of the ancient Near East. The tree was associated with palaces and kingship because the king was seen as the link between the earthly and divine realms. Through him, the gods blessed the earth with fertility.

Traditional Persian and Slavic myths both told of a tree of life that bore the seeds of all the world's plants. This tree, which looked like an ordinary tree, was guarded by an invisible dragon that the Persians called Simarghu and the Slavs called Simorg. For fear of cutting down the tree of life by accident, Slavic peoples performed sacred ceremonies before taking down a tree. The Persians cut no trees but waited for them to fall naturally. In the mythology of the Yoruba people of West Africa, a palm tree planted by the god Obatala was the first piece of vegetation on earth.

Trees—or the fruit they bore—also came to be associated with wisdom, knowledge, or hidden secrets. This meaning may have come from the symbolic connection between trees and worlds above and below human experience. The tree is a symbol of wisdom in stories about the life of Buddha, who was said to have gained spiritual enlightenment while sitting under a bodhi tree, a type of fig.

Two sacred trees—the Tree of Life and the Tree of Knowledge of Good and Evil—appear in the Near Eastern story of the Garden of Eden, told in the book of Genesis of the Bible. God ordered Adam and Eve, the first man and woman, not to eat the fruit of either tree. Disobeying, they ate fruit from the Tree of Knowledge and became aware of guilt, shame, and sin. God cast them out of the garden before they could eat the fruit of the Tree of Life, which would have made them immortal. Thereafter, they and their descendants had to live in a world that included sin and death.

A traditional Micronesian myth from the Gilbert Islands in the Pacific Ocean is similar to the biblical account of the fall from Eden. In the beginning of the world was a garden where two trees grew, guarded by an original being called Na Kaa. Men lived under one tree and gathered its fruit, while women lived apart from the men under the other tree. One day when Na Kaa was away on a trip, the men and women mingled together under one of the trees. Upon his return, Na Kaa told them that they had chosen the Tree of Death, not the Tree of Life, and from that time all people would be mortal.

† See **Names and Places** at the end of this volume for further information.

The tree of life, with sacred animals feeding on its fruit-bearing branches, is a common image in the mythology and art of the ancient Near East.

deity god or goddess

nymph minor goddess of nature, usually represented as young and beautiful

Tree Gods and Spirits

Another belief about trees sees them as embodying **deities,** spirits, or simply humans changed into trees by a special fate. Some Celtic† and other European peoples worshiped groves of trees as well as particular trees. In the religion of the Druids†, oaks were sacred. The ancient Romans associated oak trees with their sky god, Jupiter.

In Greek and Roman mythology, Dryads (also called Hamadryads) were **nymphs** who lived in trees and perished when their trees died or were cut down. A similar myth from Japan tells of a man who cherished a willow tree. One day he met a girl under the tree and married her, although her past was a mystery. When the emperor ordered the willow tree cut down to build a temple, the man's wife told him that she was the spirit of the tree, and she died as the tree fell to the ground.

Some myths tell of supernatural beings or humans who were changed into trees. In Greek mythology, the nymph Daphne turned into a laurel tree when fleeing through the forest to escape the advances of Apollo†. Lotis, another nymph who fled from unwanted advances, became the lotus tree. Other transformations symbolized eternal love. In a Greek myth, the gods turned Baucis and Philemon, a devoted old couple, into an oak and a linden tree when they died. The trees grew close together. In Japan, two pine trees growing close together were said to be faithful lovers. Tales from many cultures speak of the dead being reincarnated, or reborn, as trees, and legends and songs often tell of two trees, their branches linked or intertwined, that grow from the graves of lovers.

A Japanese myth tells of a poor elderly couple whose only joys in life were their pet dog and the beautiful blossoms of the cherry tree. After the dog found buried gold for its owners, a jealous neighbor killed the beloved animal. The old man and woman

69

buried the dog under a cherry tree and believed that the dog's spirit inhabited the tree. With wood from one of its branches, they made a mortar—a bowl for grinding grain—that magically produced plenty of flour, even in a time of famine. The same wicked neighbor burned the mortar, but the old man found that its ashes, when sprinkled on the dog's grave, caused the cherry tree to produce its lovely blossoms at any time of year. *See also* ADAM AND EVE; DRUIDS; EDEN, GARDEN OF; FLOWERS IN MYTHOLOGY; FRUIT IN MYTHOLOGY; PLANTS IN MYTHOLOGY; YGGDRASILL.

Tricksters

demigod one who is part human and part god

culture hero mythical figure who gives people the tools of civilization, such as language and fire

underworld land of the dead

Tricksters are among the most entertaining characters in world mythology. Usually male, they delight in breaking rules, boasting, and playing tricks on both humans and gods. Most tricksters are shape-changers who can take any form, though they often appear as animals. Tricksters play a prominent role in African and Native American mythologies. They can also be found in the myths of Europeans, Asians, Pacific Islanders, and the Aborigines of Australia. Certain gods, **demigods,** and heroes from around the world are described as having trickster qualities.

Tricksters' Roles. Operating outside the framework of right and wrong, tricksters do not recognize the rules of society. Their characters and actions are far from simple, however. Often childish, greedy, lustful, and even nasty, tricksters can also be friendly, helpful, clever, and wise. Sometimes they appear to be clownish, clumsy, or foolish, although they usually possess amazing powers of survival. A trickster may come to a sorry end in one story but then, after being miraculously brought back to life, reappear in other tales.

Sometimes a trickster is a creator or **culture hero** whose activities explain how some aspect of the world came into being. In northeastern America, for example, myths of the Algonquian-speaking people tell of a trickster named Gluskap. Gluskap lived in the cold north, but during a journey to the warm south, he tricked Summer, a beautiful female chieftain, into returning north with him. After she melted the cold of Winter, Gluskap let her return to her home. Maui, the trickster hero of the Polynesian Islands in the Pacific Ocean, created the world while he was fishing. He let out a long fishing line and reeled in island after island from the bottom of the ocean. Later, Maui stole fire from the **underworld** and gave it to humans.

Trickster figures appear in the myths of many Native American groups. When tricksters' pranks benefit humans, they are considered culture heroes. In stories from the Northwest Coast region, the trickster Raven recaptured the sun from a distant chief who had stolen it and left the earth in darkness.

† *See **Names and Places** at the end of this volume for further information.*

Greek mythology also includes a trickster associated with the gift of fire. The god Prometheus tricked Zeus† and the other gods into granting humans the best part of an animal killed for a sacrifice. Angry at having been tricked, Zeus refused to let humans have fire, but Prometheus stole a burning ember from the gods for people to use.

A trickster may be a go-between or messenger between the human and divine worlds. Hermes, the messenger of the gods in Greek mythology, was the god of travelers and trade but also of thieves and deceit. As a newborn child, Hermes demonstrated his cleverness by stealing cattle from Apollo†. He hid their tracks by tying tree bark to their hooves. The Norse† trickster Loki was originally a friend of the gods, but eventually they became tired of his tricks and grew to dislike him.

Eshu, a West African trickster also known as Legba, is associated with travel, commerce, and communication—or miscommunication. He creates quarrels among people or between people and gods. In one myth, he causes conflict between a man and his two wives. Disguised as a merchant, Eshu sells one of the wives a fine hat, which pleases the husband but makes the other wife jealous. Eshu then sells a more splendid hat to the second wife. The competition continues, making the husband and both wives miserable. According to another myth, the High God became so disgusted with Eshu's trickery that he left the world, ordering Eshu to remain as his link with it.

Some scholars have suggested that the trickster is one of the most ancient figures in mythology. A chaotic and disorderly character, he acts out many human urges and desires that people living in communities learn to control to maintain social order. Trickster myths, especially those in which the trickster's deeds backfire against him in some way, may have developed to teach a moral lesson about the penalties of misbehavior. Tales in which the trickster is a small but clever animal that emerges victorious teach a different lesson. They show how a seemingly powerless creature can triumph over a mighty one.

Trickster Myths. Eshu is just one of the many tricksters in African mythology. A trickster Hare appears in some myths, and tales about a trickster spider called Anansi are widespread in West Africa. Anansi is a cunning fellow who acts as God's assistant, although some stories reveal him trying to trick God.

Occasionally the trickster himself falls victim to a trick. One myth about Anansi tells how he cheated the **chameleon** out of his field. For revenge, Chameleon created a fine cloak of vines decorated with buzzing flies. Everyone wanted the cloak, but Chameleon would sell it only to the spider. The price, he told Anansi, was merely a little food, just enough to fill the tiny hole that was his storehouse. The spider agreed and sent two of his children with grain. However, Chameleon had secretly dug the deepest hole that anyone had ever seen. Anansi's children poured grain into the hole for weeks, and still it was not full. Chameleon ended

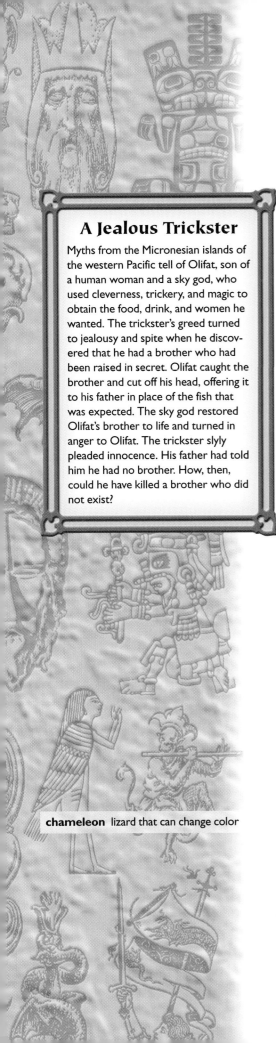

A Jealous Trickster

Myths from the Micronesian islands of the western Pacific tell of Olifat, son of a human woman and a sky god, who used cleverness, trickery, and magic to obtain the food, drink, and women he wanted. The trickster's greed turned to jealousy and spite when he discovered that he had a brother who had been raised in secret. Olifat caught the brother and cut off his head, offering it to his father in place of the fish that was expected. The sky god restored Olifat's brother to life and turned in anger to Olifat. The trickster slyly pleaded innocence. His father had told him he had no brother. How, then, could he have killed a brother who did not exist?

chameleon lizard that can change color

up with most of the spider's wealth. Anansi received only a few withered vines for his part of the bargain and fled from the mocking laughter of the people. That is why spiders hide in the corners of houses.

Tricksters figure prominently in the mythologies of Native Americans. They usually take the form of animals, although they also have some human qualities and may appear human if it suits their purposes. The most common trickster figure is Coyote, but Raven, Crow, Bluejay, Rabbit, Spider, Raccoon, Bear, and others appear in the trickster myths of some Native American groups.

A myth of the Coeur d'Alene people illustrates the sly and bumbling side of Coyote. The first people selected Coyote as their moon. But when they learned that he spied on them from the sky and told their secrets, they replaced him with a chieftain who turned the tables by keeping watch on Coyote. Then, because the sun had killed some of Coyote's children, the trickster cut out the sun's heart, plunging the world into darkness. Coyote wanted to take the heart home with him, but he kept stumbling in the dark. In the end he had to return the heart to the sun, which restored light to the world. *See also* AFRICAN MYTHOLOGY; ANANSI; ANIMALS IN MYTHOLOGY; BRER RABBIT; ESHU; HERMES; KRISHNA; LOKI; MAUI; NATIVE AMERICAN MYTHOLOGY.

Tristan and Isolde

medieval relating to the Middle Ages in Europe, a period from about A.D. 500 to 1500

chivalry rules and customs of medieval knighthood

tribute payment made by a smaller or weaker party to a more powerful one, often under the threat of force

The legend of Tristan and Isolde is the tragic tale of two lovers fated to share a forbidden but undying love. Scholars of mythology believe that the legend originated in Brittany, in western France. In time it was associated with the Arthurian legends† and became part of the mythology of **medieval** Europe, told and retold in various versions and in many languages.

The Legend. Tristan (sometimes called Tristram), the nephew of King Mark of Cornwall, was a symbol of all the virtues of **chivalry,** including bravery and honor. Some accounts also claim that he was a brilliant harp player. According to the most detailed versions of this legend, the king of Ireland sent a champion named Morholt to demand **tribute** from Cornwall, and Tristan fought Morholt in single combat. Tristan killed Morholt, leaving a broken piece of his sword in the fatal wound. The piece remained in Morholt's body when it was carried back to Ireland. Morholt had wounded Tristan as well, and when the wound did not heal, the young knight went to Ireland, in disguise, to seek help from an Irish princess named Isolde (or Iseult) who was skilled in healing.

After Isolde healed Tristan, he lingered at the Irish court for a while. On his return to Cornwall, he praised Isolde so highly that King Mark resolved to marry her. Loyal and obedient to his uncle and king, Tristan agreed to return to Ireland and seek Isolde's hand for Mark.

Back in Ireland, Tristan found that the country was being terrorized by a fearsome dragon. Tristan succeeded in killing the beast. While Isolde was nursing him back to health after the fight,

†See **Names and Places** at the end of this volume for further information.

she discovered his broken sword and realized that he was the warrior who had killed Morholt, her uncle. At first she wanted to avenge her uncle's death. However, Tristan had endeared himself to the Irish people by killing the dragon, so Isolde forgave him and agreed to marry King Mark. She set off with Tristan for Cornwall.

Many versions of the legend say that Tristan and Isolde had already begun to care for one another. Their sense of honor might have prevented them from letting their feelings show, but fate now took a hand. Isolde's mother had prepared a magical drink for Isolde to share with Mark—a potion that would make them love each other forever. During the voyage to Cornwall, Isolde and Tristan drank the potion, not knowing what it was, and fell deeply in love.

Although Isolde went through with the marriage to Mark, she could not stop loving Tristan, and he was fated to love her in return. They tried to keep their passion a secret, but eventually it became known. Some accounts of the story contain episodes of intrigue and suspense in which King Mark or various knights try to trap the lovers and obtain proof of their guilt. In the end, Tristan fled from Cornwall in despair.

By the 1200s, the legend of Tristan had been interwoven with the Arthurian legends. Tristan had become a noble knight and appeared in some of the stories about Arthur, Lancelot, and the knights of the Round Table. By this time, storytellers had also begun to portray King Mark as cruel or cowardly, perhaps to create a stronger contrast between Mark and Tristan, though in earlier versions of the legend, Mark was an honorable man.

Tristan finally settled in Brittany, where he married another Isolde, known as Isolde of the White Hands. His love for Isolde of Cornwall had never died, though. In time Tristan was wounded in battle, and his wife could not cure him. He sent for Isolde of Cornwall, hoping that she could once again heal him. He requested that the ship coming back from Cornwall should have white sails if it carried Isolde and black ones if it did not.

Tristan lay on his sickbed and waited. Finally the ship appeared on the horizon, bearing white sails. Too sick to sit up, Tristan asked about the color of the sails. Jealous of his passion for the first Isolde, his wife lied and said that they were black. Tristan fell into despair, believing that Isolde had refused to help him, and died. When Isolde arrived and learned of his death, she too died of grief. The two were buried in Cornwall. From Isolde's grave a rose tree grew, and from Tristan's came a vine that wrapped itself around the tree. Every time the vine was cut, it grew again—a sign that the two lovers could not be parted in death.

The Legacy. The legend of Tristan and Isolde, with its emphasis on a love that cannot be denied even when it leads to tragedy, has continued to appeal to artists since medieval times. It inspired three English poets of the 1800s: Matthew Arnold (*Tristram and Iseult*), Algernon Swinburne (*Tristram of Lyonesse*), and Alfred, Lord Tennyson (part of the Arthurian poem *Idylls of the King*).

Related Entries
Other entries related to Tristan and Isolde are listed at the end of this article.

Troilus and Cressida

medieval relating to the Middle Ages in Europe, a period from about A.D. 500 to 1500
epic long poem about legendary or historical heroes, written in a grand style
romance in medieval literature, a tale based on legend, love, and adventure, often set in a distant place or time

Trojan War

siege attempt to conquer a city or fortress by surrounding it with troops and cutting off supplies
epic long poem about legendary or historical heroes, written in a grand style

American poet E. A. Robinson based his *Tristram* on the legend. One of the most influential works to draw on the story was the opera *Tristan und Isolde,* by German composer Richard Wagner. ***See also*** ARTHURIAN LEGENDS; CELTIC MYTHOLOGY.

Troilus and Cressida appear in **medieval** legend as a pair of lovers. Troilus was faithful, while Cressida was not. Their story comes from the Trojan War† of Greek mythology. Virgil† mentioned Troilus in his **epic** the *Aeneid*† as one of the sons of the Trojan king Priam. He noted that Troilus was slain by the Greek hero Achilles† while driving a chariot. In the 1100s, a storyteller named Benoît de Sainte-Maure took these few items from Virgil's work and created an elaborate **romance** about Troilus. Giovanni Boccaccio and Geoffrey Chaucer wrote poems about the story in the 1300s. Around 1600, William Shakespeare used the tale as the basis for his play *Troilus and Cressida.*

According to the medieval story, Troilus fell in love with Cressida, a young Trojan woman. She was the niece of Troilus's friend Pandarus, who encouraged the relationship by carrying letters and arranging meetings. However, Cressida's father decided to side with the Greeks against his own people, and he ordered Cressida to join him in the Greek camp. There, despite her vows of loyalty to Troilus, she fell in love with a Greek soldier named Diomedes. Her faithlessness filled Troilus with rage and despair. Some versions say that he willingly died at the hands of Achilles. ***See also*** ACHILLES; PRIAM; TROJAN WAR.

In Greek mythology, the Trojan War was a legendary ten-year conflict in which Greek warriors laid **siege** to Troy, a city on the northwestern coast of Asia Minor†. Homer's† great **epic** the *Iliad* describes the activities of gods, goddesses, and human heroes during the final year of the war. Some scholars think that the story of the Trojan War may have been based on memories of distant historical events, which became myths with the passage of time.

According to these myths, the Trojan War was rooted in vanity and passion. A youth named Paris, one of the sons of King Priam of Troy, was asked to choose the fairest of three goddesses: Aphrodite†, Athena†, and Hera†. Each goddess offered Paris a special gift if he declared her the fairest. Paris selected Aphrodite, who had promised him the most beautiful woman in the world.

Aphrodite led Paris to Sparta, the home of a Greek prince named Menelaus. Helen, the wife of Menelaus, was considered the world's most beautiful woman. Paris fell in love with Helen and carried her off to Troy. Menelaus asked his brother King Agamemnon† to lead the princes and warriors of Greece against Troy to recover Helen and to punish the Trojans.

After some delays, the Greeks arrived outside Troy. They besieged the city but made little progress in the war for more than nine years. The *Iliad* takes up the story just when Agamemnon

† *See **Names and Places** at the end of this volume for further information.*

The Greeks built a large hollow horse out of wood and hid in it to get through the gates of Troy. Once inside, the Greeks set fire to the city and defeated the Trojans.

insulted Achilles†, his bravest warrior. Furious with Agamemnon, Achilles withdrew from the conflict and cursed his Greek comrades.

Meanwhile, Hector, another of Priam's sons and the leading Trojan warrior, led a force out of the besieged city to attack the Greeks. He killed Patroclus, who had borrowed the armor of his friend Achilles. Filled with grief and rage, Achilles returned to the battle and slew Hector. Then he dragged Hector's body behind his chariot, preventing the Trojans from holding a proper funeral. This dishonorable act angered the gods, who persuaded Achilles to return the body to Hector's family.

Paris killed Achilles with a well-aimed arrow, only to be killed in turn by a Greek archer. After the death of Achilles, the Greeks recognized Odysseus† as their finest warrior. The valiant Ajax, angry at being passed by, attempted to kill the other Greek leaders and finally committed suicide. Meanwhile, the clever Odysseus came up with a plan to defeat Troy by trickery rather than direct force. He instructed the Greeks to build an enormous, hollow wooden horse on wheels. Greek soldiers hid inside the horse, which was then wheeled to the gates of Troy. The Trojans awoke to find this marvel outside their gates and brought it into the city. That night the Greek soldiers climbed out of the horse and opened the city gates to admit more Greeks. Then they set Troy afire, killing Priam and his family. The term Trojan horse is used to this day to refer to something that appears to be a harmless gift but carries unsuspected danger or destruction within.

The Trojan War also provided mythological material for the Romans, who traced their ancestry to Aeneas, a Trojan nobleman who escaped the destruction of Troy. **Medieval** Europeans created new poems and legends about the Trojan War, often presenting

medieval relating to the Middle Ages in Europe, a period from about A.D. 500 to 1500

75

the Trojan point of view. A British legend, for example, claimed that Britain had been founded by descendants of Aeneas and the last Trojans. ***See also*** ACHILLES; AENEAS; AGAMEMNON; AJAX; GREEK MYTHOLOGY; HECTOR; HELEN OF TROY; HOMER; ILIAD, THE; ODYSSEUS; PARIS; PRIAM.

Trolls

Trolls were creatures in Norse† myth and legend who became part of the folklore of Scandinavia and northern Europe. Generally trolls were thought to be evil and dangerous, although sometimes they interacted peacefully with people. They were clever at building and making things of stone and metal and often lived in caves or among rocks.

Early stories described trolls as giants who lived in castles and roamed during the night. When exposed to sunlight, trolls turned to stone. The stone crags of a place called Trold-Tindterne (Troll Peaks) in central Norway are said to be two armies of trolls that once fought a great battle—until sunrise caught them and turned them to stone. Over time, trolls came to be portrayed about the size of humans or, in some cases, as small as dwarfs.

Many folktales tell of bargains between trolls and humans in which the humans must outwit the trolls or suffer sad fates. In one such story, a man named Esbern loved a girl whose father would not let his daughter marry until Esbern built a fine church. A troll agreed to build the church for Esbern on the condition that if Esbern could not discover the troll's name by the time the job was done, the troll would have Esbern's eyes and his soul. Try as he might, Esbern could not learn the troll's name. He was in despair until the girl he loved prayed for him. At that moment Esbern heard the troll's wife singing to her baby, and her song contained the name of her husband. After the people of northern Europe converted to Christianity, many of their stories featured prayer as a weapon against trolls. ***See also*** DWARFS AND ELVES; NORSE MYTHOLOGY.

Twins

As two children born on the same day to the same mother, twins have a unique sense of identity. They have more in common with one another than any two ordinary people, especially if they are identical twins. Yet twins are also separate beings who may be very different in character. Myths about twins—as partners, rivals, opposites, or halves of a whole—are rooted in this basic mystery of sameness and difference. Twins appear in the myths and legends of many cultures, but they are especially important in African and Native American mythology. In some traditions, two children may be considered twins if they are born to two sisters at the same time.

Mythical Twins. The mythology of ancient Egypt includes examples of twinship operating in different ways. According to one version of the Egyptian creation myth, the earth god Geb and the

Twins that appear in the myths and legends of Africa can bring fortune or misfortune to families and communities. These figures from Yoruba, *ibejis,* are named after the deity of twins, Ibeji.

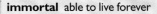

dualistic consisting of two equal and opposing forces

immortal able to live forever

underworld land of the dead

sky goddess Nut were twins and also lovers, locked together in a tight embrace. The great god Ra† separated them with air, leaving Nut arched across the heavens above Geb. Nut and Geb are complementary symbols—meaning that the two complete each other, forming a whole.

Similar myths from around the world associate twins with complementary features of the natural world, such as male and female, day and night, and sun and moon. The Xingu people of Brazil, for example, have stories about the twin brothers Kuat and Iae, who forced the vulture king Urubutsin to give light to the dark world. Kuat occupied the sun, Iae the moon. Their wakefulness keeps light in the world except for a brief time each month when they both sleep and the world experiences dark nights.

Twins can also be rivals. Egyptian mythology explores this aspect of twinship in the stories about the gods Osiris† and Set, twin sons of Nut and Geb. Set was so determined to be born first that he tore his way out of his mother's womb before he was fully formed. He hated his brother Osiris and eventually killed him. In the mythology of ancient Persia†, some accounts of Ahriman, the spirit of evil, say that he too was a twin who forced his way out of the womb so that he could be born first. Ahriman and his twin and enemy Ahura Mazda, the spirit of good, are symbols of opposing moral forces in a **dualistic** universe.

Twins often appear as partners or companions who share a bond deeper than ordinary friendship or even brotherly affection. This aspect of twinship is illustrated in the myth of Castor and Pollux (called Polydeuces by the Greeks). Some versions of their story say that although they were born to the same mother, they had different fathers. Pollux, son of Zeus†, was **immortal;** Castor, son of a human, was not. When his beloved brother was killed, Pollux gave up half of his immortality to restore Castor to life. As a result, each twin could live forever, but they had to divide their time between Mount Olympus and the **underworld.** The Greeks identified Castor and Pollux with a constellation, or star group, known as Gemini, the Twins.

Aborigines of Australia also associated this constellation with twins. According to a myth told in central Australia, twin lizards created trees, plants, and animals to fill the land. Their most heroic deed was to save a group of women from a moon spirit who wanted to mate with them. The women went into the sky as the cluster of stars now called the Pleiades, while the lizard twins became Gemini.

Because twinship is a rare and special state, some cultures said that certain gods and heroes were twins. In Greek mythology, notable sets of twins included the deities Apollo† and Artemis† and two remarkable sisters, Helen and Clytemnestra, who were also the sisters of Castor and Pollux. Some myths of community origins featured royal or even semidivine twins. The Greeks said that Amphion and Zethus, twin sons of Zeus†, had founded the city of Thebes, while the Romans claimed that the founders of their city were the twin brothers Romulus and Remus, sons of Mars†.

cosmology set of ideas about the origin, history, and structure of the universe

patron special guardian, protector, or supporter

The Stupid Twin

Many myths of the Melanesian islands in the southwest Pacific Ocean tell of twin brothers who are rivals or enemies. Often one twin is wise and the other foolish, as in the case of To Kabinana and To Karvuvu. The stupidity of To Karvuvu has led to unpleasant or dangerous things. For example, he created the shark, thinking it would help him catch more fish. Instead, the shark ate the fish—and people. When To Karvuvu's mother shed her old, wrinkled skin and became young, he wept because he could not recognize her. To calm him she put on her old skin again. Ever since that time, people have had to grow old and die.

trickster mischievous figure appearing in various forms in the folktales and mythology of many different peoples
culture hero mythical figure who gives people the tools of civilization, such as language and fire

Twinship in African Mythology. The idea of twinship is fundamental to the **cosmologies** and creation myths of some West African peoples. To the Dogon of Mali, twinship represents completeness and perfection. The symbol of this wholeness is the deity Nummo, who is really a set of twins, male and female. The act of creating the other gods and the world required the sacrifice of one part of Nummo. From that time on, all beings were either male or female, lacking Nummo's divine completeness.

The supreme creator deity of the Fon people of Benin is Mawu-Lisa, a being both male and female who is sometimes described as a pair of twins. Mawu is the moon and the female element of the deity, while Lisa is the sun and the male part. They gave birth to all of the other gods, who also were born as pairs of twins.

Among the Yoruba people of Nigeria, twins are called *ibejis* after Ibeji, the **patron** deity of twins. People believe that, depending on how they are treated, twins can bring either fortune or misfortune to their families and communities. For this reason, twins receive special attention. One myth links the origin of twins with monkeys. According to this story, monkeys destroyed a farmer's crops, so he began killing all the monkeys he could find. When the farmer's wife became pregnant, the monkeys sent two spirits into her womb. They were born as the first human twins. To keep these children from dying, the farmer had to stop killing monkeys.

Twinship in Native American Mythology. The role of twinship in Native American mythology is complex. Some pairs of twins combine heroism with the mischievous behavior of **tricksters.** Occasionally, twins represent opposing forces of good and evil. The Huron people of northeastern North America tell of Ioskeha and Tawiskara, twins who dueled to rule the world. The evil Tawiskara, who fought his way out of the womb, used a twig as his weapon against his brother, while Ioskeha used the horn of a stag. Ioskeha, a positive creative force, won the conflict. In the same way, Gluskap, the creator god and **culture hero** of many northeastern myths, had to defeat Malsum, his evil twin, who was the source of all harmful things and the ruler of demons. In Iroquois mythology, Good Mind helps his grandmother, the Woman Who Fell From the Sky, place useful and beautiful items on the earth. His twin, Warty One, creates unpleasant things, such as mosquitoes and thorny bushes.

Rather than enemies, twins in Native American mythology are often partners in a task or a quest. In myths from the Pacific Northwest, the twins Enumclaw and Kapoonis sought to obtain power over fire and rock from the spirits. Their activities became so threatening that the sky god made them into spirits themselves. Enumclaw ruled lightning, and Kapoonis controlled thunder.

Hunahpú and Xbalanqúe, Hero Twins of Mayan mythology, descended into the underworld to restore their father to life. They then escaped from the lords of the underworld by outwitting them. Masewi and Oyoyewi, culture heroes in the myths of the

†*See **Names and Places** at the end of this volume for further information.*

Acoma Indians of the American Southwest, made a journey to their father, the sun. The theme of twins in search of their father also appears in the myth of Ariconte and Tamendonare of the Tupinamba people of Brazil. Setting out on a quest to learn their father's identity, these twin sons faced many dangerous trials. Each twin died once, only to be brought back to life by his brother. In the end, they learned that they had different fathers, one immortal and one mortal. Because the twins did not know which of them had the immortal father, they protected one another forever.

Navajo myths tell of Monster Slayer (Naayéé'neizghání) and his twin brother Child of Water (Tó bájísh chíní). Their father carried the sun across the sky and was too busy to pay attention to his sons. One day the twins went in search of him. After enduring a series of ordeals, they at last found their father, and he equipped them to roam the world fighting monsters. **See also AHRIMAN; AHURA MAZDA; CASTOR AND POLLUX; CLYTEMNESTRA; HELEN OF TROY; HUNAHPÚ AND XBALANQÚE; MASEWI AND OYOYEWI; NUMMO; OSIRIS; ROMULUS AND REMUS; SET.**

Tyr

In Norse† mythology, Tyr was worshiped as a god of war, justice, and order. One of his roles was to guarantee that contracts and oaths were not broken.

Although Tyr appears in very few legends, the best-known story about him involves the fierce wolf Fenrir that no chain could hold. The supreme god Odin ordered the dwarfs to make a magical ribbon so strong that Fenrir could not break it. Fenrir was suspicious when the gods wanted to tie the ribbon around him. But he allowed himself to be bound after brave Tyr put his hand in the wolf's mouth. However, when Fenrir realized that he had been tricked, he bit off Tyr's hand.

Early Germanic peoples associated Tyr with Mars, the Roman god of war. The third day of the week, known as *dies Martis* (Mars' Day) in Latin, became known as *Tyrsdagr* to the Norse and entered English as Tuesday. **See also FENRIR; MARS; NORSE MYTHOLOGY.**

Ulysses

The Greek hero Odysseus† was known to the Romans as Ulixes, which became Ulysses in English. This name has been used in English translations of Homer's† *Iliad* and *Odyssey* since the 1600s and in other literature based on the life of Odysseus.

In Dante's *The Divine Comedy,* written in the late 1200s, a character named Ulysses told of a voyage beyond the Pillars of Hercules—two peaks at the western entrance to the Mediterranean. His goal was to explore the unknown world, and he and his crew sailed westward for five months. Just as they sighted land, a fierce storm destroyed their ship and killed them.

In the literature of the Middle Ages, Ulysses was often portrayed as a liar and a rogue. In his poem "The Rape of Lucrece," Shakespeare

referred to "sly Ulysses." In the mid-1800s, Alfred, Lord Tennyson portrayed the hero's final years in his poem *Ulysses.*

James Joyce's novel *Ulysses,* written in 1922, is based on the *Odyssey.* Each chapter in the novel takes a different episode from Homer's work to document a single hour of a day in Dublin. **See also** ODYSSEUS; ODYSSEY, THE.

Underworld

supernatural related to forces beyond the normal world; magical or miraculous

shaman person thought to possess spiritual and healing powers

epic long poem about legendary or historical heroes, written in a grand style

From all parts of the world come myths and legends about the underworld, a mysterious and shadowy place beyond ordinary human experience. The underworld is the realm of the dead, the destination of human souls in the afterlife. In some traditions, it is also the home of nonhuman, **supernatural,** or otherworldly beings such as fairies, demons, giants, and monsters. Although usually portrayed as a terrifying, dangerous, or unpredictable place, the underworld appears as a source of growth, life, and rebirth in some myths. Many descriptions of the underworld include elements of earthly life, such as powerful rulers and palaces.

The most common idea of the underworld is that it lies beneath the everyday world. The passage from this world to the other may begin by descending into a cave, well, or pit. However, the distance between the two worlds is more than physical, and the spiritual journey involved often includes great peril. The souls of the dead are the principal travelers, but sometimes living heroes, mystics, and **shamans** also make the journey.

The Land of the Dead. Many cultures believe that after death the soul travels to the underworld. In some traditions the passage to or through the underworld is part of a process that involves judgment of the individual's deeds when alive, and perhaps punishment for evil deeds. In others the underworld is simply the destination of all the dead, good and bad alike.

Some of the earliest descriptions of the underworld occur in myths from ancient Mesopotamia†. One tells how the fertility goddess Inanna, later known as Ishtar, descends into the kingdom of the dead, ruled by her sister Ereshkigal. Trying to overthrow Ereshkigal, Inanna is killed. The other gods convince Ereshkigal to release Inanna, but Inanna cannot leave the underworld without finding someone to take her place. She determines that her husband, Dumuzi or Tammuz, should be her substitute. Some scholars believe that this myth is related to the annual death and rebirth of vegetation.

The underworld Inanna visits is the same as that described in the Mesopotamian **epic** of Gilgamesh, in which the character Enkidu has a vision of himself among the dead. The underworld described is a dim, dry, dreary place called the House of Darkness, a house that none who enter leave. The dead dwell in darkness, eating dust and clay. Although recognizable as individuals, they are pale and powerless shadows of their former selves.

This Semitic† image of the underworld appears in early Jewish mythology. The Jewish underworld was Sheol, which means "pit."

*† See **Names and Places** at the end of this volume for further information.*

The idea of the afterlife played a central role in Egyptian religion. When humans died, their souls began a difficult journey through the underworld. This tomb painting of the 1200s B.C. shows Ramses I surrounded by deities in the underworld.

It held all the dead who had ever lived. Over time, as the idea of judgment in the afterlife took root in Jewish and then Christian belief, the early, neutral concept of the underworld changed. Sheol became a place of punishment and torment for the souls of sinners.

The ancient Greek vision of the underworld was, at first, much like that of the early Semitic cultures. All the dead went to the same place—a vague, shadowy underworld populated by the ghosts, or shades, of the dead. This realm is sometimes called Hades, after the god who ruled it. Gradually the underworld of Greek and then Roman mythology became more elaborate. The kingdom of Hades was said to lie either beyond the ocean or deep within the earth, separated from the world of the living by five rivers: Acheron (woe), Styx (hate), Lethe (forgetfulness), Cocytus (wailing), and Phlegethon (fire). Cerberus, a fierce, three-headed, doglike monster, guarded the entrance to the underworld, which consisted of various regions. The souls of the good dwelled in the Elysian Fields or Islands of the Blessed, while those who deserved punishment went to a deep pit called Tartarus.

Mesoamerica cultural region consisting of southern Mexico and northern regions of Central America

To the Maya of **Mesoamerica,** the underworld was a dreadful place, but not one limited to sinners. Only people who died a violent death went to a heaven in the afterlife. Everyone else entered Xibalba, the underworld, whose name meant "place of fright." Any cave or body of still water was an entrance to Xibalba.

The dead were not confined to the underworld forever. In the Mayan sacred book *Popol Vuh,* the Hero Twins Hunahpú and Xbalanqúe outwitted the lords of Xibalba and left the land of death. The souls of kings and nobles could also escape from Xibalba if they were summoned by living relatives during the Serpent Vision ceremony.

The Aztecs of central Mexico believed that the underworld consisted of eight layers, each with its own dangers, such as drowning or sharp blades. Souls descended through the layers until they reached Mictlan, the bottommost part of the underworld.

The underworld of Japanese mythology was Yomi, land of night or gloom. It was empty until the creator goddess Izanami died after giving birth to the god of fire. The maggots that appeared in her dead body grew into a host of demons who populated Yomi and tormented the souls of the wicked. Although Yomi was said to be a dark region of barren plains and lonely tunnels, artists often portrayed it as an underground palace crowded with the dead and

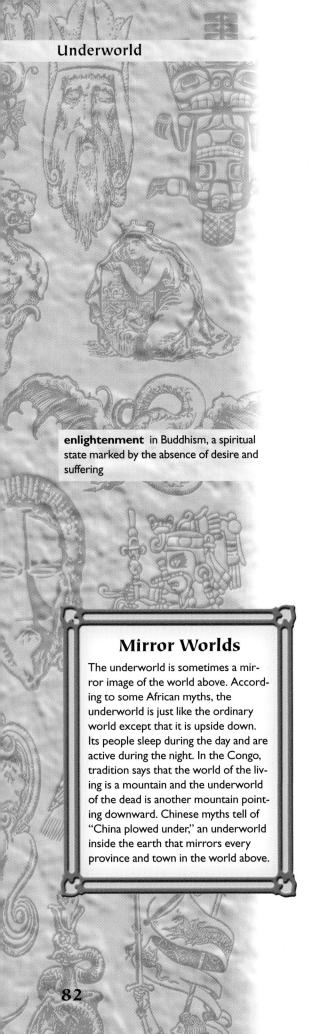

enlightenment in Buddhism, a spiritual state marked by the absence of desire and suffering

Mirror Worlds

The underworld is sometimes a mirror image of the world above. According to some African myths, the underworld is just like the ordinary world except that it is upside down. Its people sleep during the day and are active during the night. In the Congo, tradition says that the world of the living is a mountain and the underworld of the dead is another mountain pointing downward. Chinese myths tell of "China plowed under," an underworld inside the earth that mirrors every province and town in the world above.

demons. Also there was Emma-Ô (the Japanese version of Yama, the Buddhist god of death), who judged the souls as they arrived in Yomi.

The Journey to the Underworld. Many myths tell of heroes who entered the underworld while still alive. Those who survived the ordeals of the journey often returned to the living world transformed by the experience, perhaps bearing special wisdom or treasure.

Some heroes wished to rescue or reclaim a loved one who had died. In Greek mythology, Demeter went down to the underworld to try to bring back her daughter, Persephone, whom Hades had carried off. The Greek hero Orpheus† traveled to the underworld in search of his wife Eurydice.

Chinese Buddhist mythology tells of a hero named Radish, a disciple of Buddha. Before leaving on a journey, Radish gave his mother, Lady Leek Stem, money for begging monks. The mother failed to give the money to the monks, but she lied to her son and said that she had done so. When Lady Leek Stem died, she went to hell.

Radish became so holy that he was made a saint named Mulian. With Mulian's **enlightenment** came the knowledge of his mother's torment. He went to hell to save her, although Yama, the king of hell, warned him that no one had the power to change a sinner's punishment. On his way Mulian had to travel past 50 demons, each with the head of an animal and swords for teeth. By waving a wand that Buddha had given him, he was able to make them disappear. Finally Mulian found his mother, nailed to a bed. But he could not release her; only Buddha could change a sinner's fate. Mulian asked Buddha for mercy for his mother, and after the proper prayers Buddha released Lady Leek Stem from hell.

The Ashanti people of Africa have a myth about Kwasi Benefo, who made a journey to the underworld. Kwasi Benefo married four women in turn, and each one died. Miserable and alone, he decided to go to Asamando, the land of the dead, to seek his lost loves. He went to the place of burial and then beyond it, passing through a dark, silent, trackless forest. He came to a river. On the far side sat Amokye, the old woman who greets dead women's souls. She felt sorry for Kwasi Benefo and allowed him to cross the river, though normally the living are forbidden to enter Asamando. Soon Kwasi Benefo found the invisible spirits of his wives. They told him to marry again, promising that his fifth wife would live and that they would be waiting for him in the underworld when his time came to die. Kwasi Benefo fell asleep and awoke in the forest. He brought from the underworld the precious gift of peace of mind, which allowed him to marry and live a normal life for the rest of his days.

The Otherworld. In some myths the underworld is a kind of alternative reality, a land not merely of the human dead but of different beings who live according to different rules. Celtic† mythology contains many accounts of an otherworldly realm. Its

*†See **Names and Places** at the end of this volume for further information.*

location was said to be far away on remote islands or lying beneath the sea or the ground. Certain caves or hills were believed to be entrances to this otherworld.

In Wales the otherworld was called Annwn, which means "notworld." It had a number of different sides. Primarily, the otherworld was the kingdom of the dead, and its grim ruler was known as Arawn to the Welsh and Donn to the Irish. However, the otherworld could also be a joyous and peaceful place or a source of wisdom, magic, and enchantment. The fairies, demons, spirits, and other supernatural beings who lived there were neither purely good nor purely evil. Depending on the circumstances, they could bring humans either harm or good fortune.

Celtic folklore is filled with legends of living people who entered the otherworld. Some went voluntarily, like King Arthur of Britain, who led an army into Annwn to capture a magical **cauldron.** Others were lured into the otherworld by fairies, sometimes in human or animal form. The theme of a human straying into the otherworld appears in many European fairy tales that draw on the old notion of the underworld as a supernatural realm. In such stories, a human who ate or drank while in the otherworld could never leave. Those who resisted food and managed to leave found that time had different meanings in the two worlds. After spending a single night in the otherworld, a person might return to the world above to find that years had passed.

cauldron large kettle

The Source of Life. The underworld does not always represent the kingdom of the gloomy dead or the home of dangerous beings. In some myths it serves as the point of contact between the surface world of the living and the earth's powerful creative forces. Among the Ibo people of Western Africa, Ala, the goddess of the underworld, is also the earth goddess who protects the harvest, which emerges from the ground. Ala receives the dead—burial is thought to be placing the dead in her pocket or womb. However, Ala also ensures life by making people and animals fertile.

The creation myths of many Native American cultures say that people and animals emerged from an underworld or series of underworlds. In these stories the underworld is a womb in which life is nurtured or prepared until the time is right for it to enter the world. One of many emergence myths is told by the Zuni, who say that the Ahuyuuta twins were sent deep into the earth by their

Yama, the Buddhist god of death, judged souls as they arrived in the Japanese underworld called Yomi, a dark land of gloom.

83

father the sun god to guide unformed creatures up to the daylight. Once above the ground, the creatures changed into human beings.

According to the Jicarilla Apache of New Mexico, in the beginning all people, animals, and plants lived in the dark underworld. Those who wanted light played a game with those who liked darkness. The light-lovers won, and the sun and stars appeared. Then the sun, looking through a hole in the roof of the underworld, saw the surface of the earth, which was covered with water.

Eager to reach this hole in the underworld, the people built four great hills that grew upward. But after girls picked the flowers from the hills, the hills stopped rising. Then the people climbed to the roof on ladders made of buffalo horns. They sent the moon and sun through the hole to light the world and dispatched the winds to blow away the water. Next they sent out animals. Last of all, the people climbed up into the new world. Once they reached the surface, they spread out in four directions. Only the Jicarilla stayed in the original homeland near the hole that led up from the underworld. *See also* AFTERLIFE; ELYSIUM; HADES; HELL; INANNA; IZANAGI AND IZANAMI; ORPHEUS; PERSEPHONE; SHEOL; STYX; XIBALBA.

Unicorn

medieval relating to the Middle Ages in Europe, a period from about A.D. 500 to 1500

The word *unicorn* comes from the Latin for "one-horned" and refers to an imaginary beast that appears in the legends of China, India, Mesopotamia†, and Europe. Since **medieval** times the unicorn has often been portrayed as a horse with a single horn growing from its forehead. Descriptions of the animal in various sources differ somewhat, but they all agree on the horn. Some images of unicorns were probably based on real animals, such as the one-horned rhinoceros or the narwhal—a small whale with a single long tooth or tusk that resembles a spiral ivory horn.

In Chinese tradition, the unicorn was one of four magical or spiritual creatures—along with the phoenix, tortoise, and dragon—that were regarded as signs of good fortune. The appearance of a unicorn signaled the birth or death of a great person; one was said to have appeared when Confucius, a famous wise man, was born.

The Western image of the unicorn comes in part from the Hebrew Bible. During its translation into Greek, a Hebrew word for "wild ox" was changed to a Greek word that people interpreted as a reference to either a unicorn or a rhinoceros. Around 400 B.C., the Greek historian Ctesias wrote of a wild beast in India that had a single horn and fought elephants. It was probably the rhinoceros, though later writers developed an image that much more closely resembled a horned horse.

By the Middle Ages, Europeans had come to believe that these horselike unicorns really existed in remote parts of the world. Among the legends linked to them was the belief that water touched by a unicorn's horn became safe for animals and people to drink. From this tradition developed the idea that powdered unicorn horn offered protection against poison and possibly cured disease as well. Rich and important people treasured horns

Unicorns are imaginary beasts that appear in legends from China, India, Mesopotamia, and Europe. This image of a unicorn is located on the Babylon Gate, one of the eight fortified gates that enclosed the ancient city of Babylon.

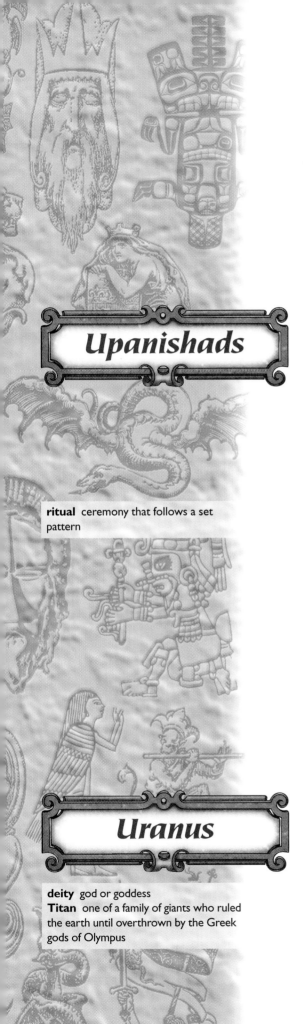

and powders said to have come from unicorns. Some kings, fearing that rivals might try to poison them, drank from vessels that they believed to be unicorn horns.

Although unicorns were thought to be fierce fighters, they were also symbols of purity. Perhaps this was because the ancient Greeks and Romans had associated them with virgin goddesses such as Artemis, whose chariot was said to be drawn by eight unicorns. According to tradition, one way to capture a unicorn was to send a very young virgin into the forest. The unicorn would be attracted to her and would rest its head in her lap, at which point a hunter could catch the animal. *See also* ANIMALS IN MYTHOLOGY.

Upanishads

ritual ceremony that follows a set pattern

The *Upanishads* are a collection of sacred texts that form one of the foundations of Hindu religious thought. The most important of these texts, written between about 600 and 300 B.C., deal primarily with the nature of humans and the universe. Originally passed on orally, these works were eventually collected and written down by wise men called *rishis*.

The texts of the *Upanishads* are said to hold the "hidden meanings" of the religious practices and ideas presented in the Vedas, an older collection of sacred texts. Hindu beliefs based on the *Upanishads* are known as the Vedanta, which means that they came after the Vedas.

Rather than focusing on religious **ritual** and practice, the *Upanishads* are philosophical works that explore the nature of reality and meaning of life. One of their central teachings is the idea that behind the everyday world is a timeless, unchanging reality or spirit, called brahman, that is identical to the inner essence, or atman, of the human being. Unity with brahman and knowledge of the hidden reality behind existence can be achieved through yoga, which involves philosophical investigation and the highly disciplined practice of meditation.

The *Upanishads* also present the Hindu idea of reincarnation, in which individuals are reborn again and again as other living creatures. The main purpose of the *Upanishads* is to help individuals gain the mystical knowledge that will release them from this continuing cycle of death and rebirth. *See also* BRAHMA; HINDUISM AND MYTHOLOGY; RIG-VEDA; VEDAS.

Uranus

deity god or goddess
Titan one of a family of giants who ruled the earth until overthrown by the Greek gods of Olympus

Uranus, who represented the sky, was one of the original **deities** of Greek mythology. He was the son of Gaia, the earth, who also became his wife. Together they had many children, including the **Titans** and the Cyclopes†.

Uranus, however, detested his children. As soon as they were born, he forced them into Tartarus, a dark place deep beneath the surface of the earth. Gaia asked her children to stop Uranus, but only her son Cronus came to her aid. Cronus cut off his father's sex organs and threw them into the sea. According to myth, Aphrodite† was born from the foam where they landed.

85

Uranus became the sky that surrounds the earth, and Cronus replaced his father as king of the universe. But Cronus was later defeated by his son Zeus† who, together with Hera† and other Olympian gods, overthrew the Titans and took their place ruling the universe. ***See also* CRONUS; TITANS.**

Utnapishtim

epic long poem about legendary or historical heroes, written in a grand style

In the mythology of the ancient Near East, Utnapishtim was the heroic survivor of a great flood. His story, told in the Babylonian **epic** *Gilgamesh*, is similar to the biblical account of Noah and the Ark. In the Babylonian story, some of the gods decided to send a flood to destroy humanity. However, Ea, the god of wisdom and water, warned Utnapishtim of the coming flood and told him to build a ship for himself and his family. The ship was to be loaded with various possessions as well as with plants and animals of every kind.

After Utnapishtim completed the ship, it began to rain. The rain continued for seven days and flooded the earth. When the rain stopped, the ship became grounded on a mountain surrounded by water. Several days passed. On the seventh day, Utnapishtim sent a dove to search for dry land. The bird came back exhausted, having found no place to rest. The next day he sent a swallow, but it returned as well. On the ninth day, Utnapishtim sent a raven. When the raven failed to come back, Utnapishtim knew that it had found dry land.

immortality ability to live forever

Utnapishtim released the animals and then offered a sacrifice to the gods. The god Enlil was furious that anyone had escaped the flood, but Ea defended Utnapishtim and calmed the angry god. Impressed by the virtue and wisdom of Utnapishtim, Enlil rewarded him and his wife with **immortality.** They became the ancestors of a new human race.

In the *Epic of Gilgamesh,* the hero Gilgamesh visits Utnapishtim to learn the secret of living forever. Utnapishtim tells Gilgamesh his story and explains that only the gods can grant immortality. ***See also* ENLIL; FLOODS; GILGAMESH; NOAH; SEMITIC MYTHOLOGY.**

Valentine, St.

patron special guardian, protector, or supporter
martyr person who suffers or is put to death for a belief
pagan term used by early Christians to describe non-Christians and non-Christian beliefs

According to tradition, St. Valentine is the **patron** saint of courtship, travelers, and young people. One story says that he was a Roman priest who became a **martyr** because he helped persecuted Christians around A.D. 270. Sent to prison, he restored the sight of a blind girl, who fell in love with him. According to another tale, Valentine was a young man awaiting execution. He loved the jailer's daughter and signed a farewell message to her "From your Valentine."

Early celebrations in honor of St. Valentine took place in the middle of February, around the time of an ancient Roman **pagan** festival known as the Lupercalia. It was customary for men to draw the name of a young girl from a box and celebrate the festival with her. The Christian church substituted names of saints for

*†See **Names and Places** at the end of this volume for further information.*

the women, and individuals who picked them were supposed to draw inspiration from the lives of the saints.

During the Middle Ages, St. Valentine's feast day on February 14 became known as a day for lovers. The custom of sending valentines to a loved one on St. Valentine's Day may have come from the belief that birds begin to choose their mates on that day.

Valhalla

In Norse† mythology, Valhalla—which means hall of the dead—was the great hall of the god Odin†. It was located in Asgard, the home of the gods of war and the sky. According to legend, the heroic warriors slain in battle gathered in Valhalla. There they enjoyed a glorious afterlife and awaited Ragnarok, a time of great destruction when they would join the gods to wage a final battle against the forces of evil. Valhalla had more than 640 doors, each wide enough to allow hundreds of warriors to leave at the first sign of threat. Filled with shields and armor, the enormous hall was also the haunt of wolves, ravens, a boar that could be eaten and brought back to life, and a goat that provided an unlimited supply of an alcoholic drink called mead.

The Valkyries, the battle maidens of Odin, selected the warriors worthy enough to live in Valhalla. When these warriors died, they entered the palace and their wounds were healed miraculously. They spent their days feasting and improving their battle skills in preparation for Ragnarok. Those warriors who were killed during practice each day were brought back to life and healed each evening. *See also* **Heroes; Norse Mythology; Odin; Ragnarok; Valkyries.**

Valkyries

supernatural related to forces beyond the normal world; magical or miraculous

Female spirits in Norse† mythology, the Valkyries were servants of the god Odin†. Originally, the Valkyries were fierce creatures who took part in battles and devoured bodies of the dead on battlefields. They later emerged as beautiful female warriors—clad in armor on horseback—who rode over battlefields selecting the bravest slain warriors to enter Valhalla†, Odin's great hall in Asgard. During battles the Valkyries carried out Odin's commands, bringing either victory or defeat according to his wishes. After leading slain warriors to Valhalla, the Valkyries waited on them, serving them food and drink.

In several myths, the Valkyries appeared as giant beings with **supernatural** powers who could cause a rain of blood to fall upon the land or row ships across the sky on rivers of blood. Some Valkyries caused warriors to die, while others served as protectors, guarding the lives of those most dear to them. Valkyries were often shown as wives of heroes. Brunhilde, one of the most famous Valkyries in mythology, disobeyed Odin and was placed in an enchanted sleep within a wall of fire as punishment. *See also* **Brunhilde; Norse Mythology; Odin; Valhalla.**

Vampires

heretic person whose beliefs are contrary to church doctrine

In European folklore, a vampire is a corpse that rises from the grave and sucks blood from the living. According to some accounts, the dead become vampires because demons or evil spirits enter their bodies. Vampires are also said to be dead werewolves, witches, criminals, suicides, and **heretics.** In some legends, the victims of vampire attacks turn into vampires themselves.

Much vampire folklore originated in Hungary and the Slavic areas of eastern Europe and western Russia. The most famous of all vampires, Dracula, is associated with the Transylvania region of Romania.

The principal characteristic of the vampire is that when buried it does not decay like a normal corpse. Instead, it leaves the grave at night to search for victims. According to tradition, a vampire remains active as long as it can obtain blood. It avoids the sun—some sources say that direct sunlight will kill a vampire—and often sleeps in its coffin by day. Methods of killing a vampire include driving a wooden stake through its heart, cutting off its head, and burning it. Garlic and Christian crosses are thought to offer some protection from a vampire's attack. *See also* DRACULA; MONSTERS; WEREWOLVES; WITCHES AND WIZARDS.

Vampires are bodies that rise from their graves and suck the blood from the living. Dracula, the most famous vampire, appears in this photograph from a movie scene.

†*See* **Names and Places** *at the end of this volume for further information.*

Varuna

deity god or goddess
morality ideas about what is right and wrong in human conduct

immortality ability to live forever

One of the oldest gods in Hindu mythology, Varuna was originally a creator and the ruler of the sky. In the Vedas—the sacred texts of ancient India—he was a supreme, all-knowing **deity** who enforced the laws of the universe and human **morality.** He ruled the gods known as the Adityas. In later Hindu belief, Varuna became the god of water and was associated with oceans and rivers.

According to the Vedas, Varuna created the heavens, the earth, and the air. He was responsible for causing rain to fall, rivers to flow, and winds to blow. The god watched over his creations from a golden palace in the sky.

Varuna was the source of all truth and justice. He judged the actions of humans and punished those who broke the laws of the gods by tying them up in a rope that he carried with him at all times. This all-knowing deity also controlled the fate of humans and had the power to grant or deny **immortality** to some beings. In addition, Varuna guarded the kingdom of the dead, along with Yama, the god of the dead.

In later Hindu belief, Varuna lost his supreme authority to the god Indra. Other gods took over many of Varuna's roles. Considered guardian of the west and ruler of the oceans and rivers, he became a minor deity. In Hindu art, Varuna is usually shown riding the Makara, a fantastic sea monster with the head of a deer and the legs of an antelope. *See also* HINDUISM AND MYTHOLOGY; INDRA; VEDAS.

Vedas

seer one who can predict the future

ritual ceremony that follows a set pattern

incantation chant, often part of a magical formula or spell

The Vedas, one of the foundations of Hindu religion and mythology, are a collection of ancient sacred texts. They are considered to be divine communications from the god Brahma† to **seers** called *rishis*. Composed between 1500 and 1000 B.C., the Vedas were passed on orally for hundreds of years before being written down in Sanskrit, an ancient Indo-European language.

The Vedas consist of hymns and verses directed toward various gods and goddesses as well as ceremonial texts, magical spells, and curses. Many of the hymns, or mantras, are chanted or recited during religious **rituals.** Although the Vedas are not true myths or stories about the gods, they contain information that serves as the basis for mythology.

Four collections of texts make up the Vedas. The *Rig-Veda* is the oldest and most important collection; the other three are the *Sama-Veda,* the *Yajur-Veda,* and the *Atharva-Veda.* The first three, known as the *trayi-vidya* (threefold knowledge), are concerned with public religious belief and ritual. The last collection, the *Atharva-Veda,* is more private in nature, dealing mainly with folk beliefs, such as magical spells and **incantations.** Because of their ancient authority and sacredness, the Vedas remain a central element in Hinduism. *See also* BRAHMA; HINDUISM AND MYTHOLOGY; RIG-VEDA.

89

Venus

deity god or goddess

Venus, the goddess of love and beauty, played an important role in Roman mythology. She began as a minor agricultural **deity** of ancient Italy associated with gardens and fields. Temples to Venus were built in several early Latin cities.

As Romans became familiar with the Greek myths of Aphrodite†, they increasingly identified Venus with that goddess. They also linked Venus with other foreign goddesses, such as the Babylonian Ishtar. One result of this connection was the naming of the planet Venus, which Babylonian astronomers had earlier associated with Ishtar.

The first temples dedicated to Venus appeared in Rome in the 200s B.C. Others followed, and in 46 B.C., Julius Caesar dedicated a new temple to Venus in her role as Genetrix, or "one who gave birth." By this time the goddess had taken on special importance to Romans. According to a myth in Virgil's *Aeneid*†, Venus's love affair with a Trojan man named Anchises produced a son, Aeneas, who survived the Trojan War†. Venus helped Aeneas escape from the ruins of Troy and reach Italy. Later when Aeneas was fighting an Italian warrior named Turnus, his spear became stuck in a tree. Venus saved Aeneas by returning the spear to him. Aeneas's descendants went on to found Rome.

Venus, the Roman goddess of love and beauty, was often identified with the Greek goddess Aphrodite. Sandro Botticelli's painting *The Birth of Venus* from the mid-1480s shows the goddess rising from a seashell.

†*See **Names and Places** at the end of this volume for further information.*

medieval relating to the Middle Ages in Europe, a period from about A.D. 500 to 1500

In this mythological interpretation of Roman history, the goddess Venus took a direct hand in establishing the Roman people and state. She was especially important to a noble family called the Iulii, who claimed to be descended from Aeneas. Julius Caesar belonged to this family, and he and his heirs—including the emperors Augustus and Nero—considered Venus to be one of their ancestors.

Like Aphrodite, Venus was married to the god of fire, known to the Romans as Vulcan. However, she had love affairs with other gods and men, notably Mars† and Adonis. She was the mother of Cupid, known to the Greeks as Eros.

By early **medieval** times, European Christians had come to view Venus as a symbol of the darker side of sensual and sexual pleasure. In the centuries that followed, however, a more balanced view of Venus emerged. Literature and artworks such as Botticelli's *The Birth of Venus* (ca. 1482) portray her as the embodiment of female beauty and fertility. *See also* ADONIS; AENEAS; AENEID, THE; APHRODITE; EROS; GREEK MYTHOLOGY; MARS; ROMAN MYTHOLOGY; VULCAN.

Vesta

immortality ability to live forever
Titan one of a family of giants who ruled the earth until overthrown by the Greek gods of Olympus

In Roman mythology, Vesta was the virgin goddess of the hearth. Worshiped in every Roman household, Vesta served as a symbol of home and family as well as the guardian of the sacred fire in her temples. As keeper of this flame—a source of life and **immortality**—the goddess played a prominent role in Roman culture.

Vesta was an important figure in Greek mythology as well. Known as Hestia, she was the daughter of the **Titans** Cronus† and Rhea and the sister of the gods Zeus†, Poseidon†, Hades†, Demeter†, and Hera†. The Greeks kept her sacred fire burning in their capital cities and took it with them when they founded new colonies.

The Romans believed that their legendary ancestor Aeneas† had brought the sacred fire to Italy from Troy†. They thought that if Vesta's fire went out, Rome would experience a great disaster. Virgin priestesses known as the Vestals kept the fire burning constantly in the Temple of Vesta in Rome. Vestals who lost their virginity, and thus dishonored the goddess, were buried alive. Each year on March 1, Vesta's fire was renewed during a ceremony, and on June 9, the Romans held a festival in her honor called the Vestalia. *See also* FIRE; GREEK MYTHOLOGY; ROMAN MYTHOLOGY.

Vishnu

deity god or goddess

Known as the preserver, Vishnu is one of three supreme Hindu **deities,** along with Brahma and Shiva. Vishnu's role is to protect humans and to restore order to the world. His presence is found in every object and force in creation, and some Hindus recognize him as the divine being from which all things come. Vishnu appears in a number of Hindu texts, including the *Rig-Veda,* the *Mahabharata,* and the *Ramayana.*

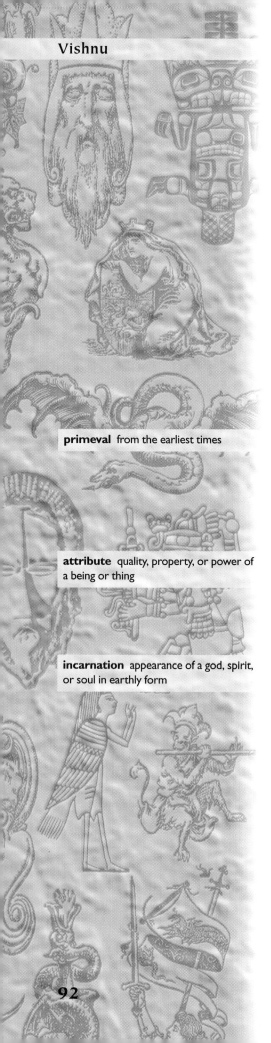

primeval from the earliest times

attribute quality, property, or power of a being or thing

incarnation appearance of a god, spirit, or soul in earthly form

In many Hindu stories, Vishnu helps humans and restores order to the world. While he sleeps, Vishnu is protected by Shesha, king of the serpents called Nagas. This illustration shows Shesha supporting Vishnu and his wife Lakshimi over the cosmic ocean.

Early Roles. In the Vedas, a collection of ancient sacred texts that includes the *Rig-Veda,* Vishnu is only a minor god. Associated with the power of light, he floated on the surface of the **primeval** ocean on top of a thousand-headed snake called Shesha. Vishnu's most famous feat in the Vedas was to take the three steps that measured the extent of the world, an act that was part of creation. Some stories credit Vishnu with a major role in creation; others say he assisted the god Indra. Early myths also portray Vishnu as a messenger between humans and the gods. Over time, the character of Vishnu combined the **attributes** of a number of heroes and gods, and he eventually became one of the most important and popular Hindu deities.

Forms of Vishnu. According to Hindu mythology, Vishnu comes to earth in a variety of animal and human forms called avatars. These avatars are **incarnations** of the god that contain part of his divine spirit and power. Hindus believe that an avatar of Vishnu appears whenever the world or humans are in danger, and in this way, the god helps to overcome evil, bring justice, and restore order.

Vishnu had ten principal avatars. The first, Matsya, was a fish that saved the first human, Manu, from a great flood by leading his ship to safety. Kurma, the second avatar, was the tortoise that recovered some precious objects that the gods had lost during another great flood. Also saved from the flood was Lakshmi, a goddess of fortune and beauty who became Vishnu's wife. Vishnu appeared on earth a third time as Varaha, the boar. Varaha rid the world of a demon giant named Hiranyaksha, who had dragged the earth to the bottom of the ocean and threatened to keep it there. After a thousand-year struggle, Varaha killed the demon.

Vishnu's fourth avatar, the man lion Narasinha, freed the world from another demon, Hiranyakashipu, who had forbidden worship of the gods. When the evil king Bali gained control of the

† *See **Names and Places** at the end of this volume for further information.*

world, Vishnu appeared on earth a fifth time as Vamana, the dwarf. Vamana persuaded Bali to give him whatever land he could cover in three steps. The dwarf then changed into a giant, and his steps extended over both heaven and earth. Vishnu's sixth avatar was Parasurama, a young man who freed the Hindu priests from a class of warriors known as the Kshatriyas.

Vishnu's most popular and well-known avatars were Rama and Krishna, the great heroes of the epics the *Ramayana* and *Mahabharata*. Rama, the seventh avatar, saved humans from the demon king Ravana, while Krishna rid the world of many demons and took part in a long struggle against the forces of evil. The ninth avatar of Vishnu was the Buddha, the religious leader whose beliefs weakened the opponents of the gods and who founded the Buddhist faith. Vishnu's tenth avatar, Kalki, has not yet arrived on earth. He will come one day, mounted on a white horse, to oversee the final destruction of the wicked, restore purity, renew creation, and bring forth a new era of harmony and order. ***See also*** ANIMALS IN MYTHOLOGY; BRAHMA; BUDDHISM AND MYTHOLOGY; DEVILS AND DEMONS; FLOODS; HINDUISM AND MYTHOLOGY; INDRA; MAHABHARATA, THE; RAMA; RAMAYANA, THE; RIG-VEDA; SHIVA; VEDAS.

Vulcan

patron special guardian, protector, or supporter

nymph minor goddess of nature, usually represented as young and beautiful

invincible too powerful to be conquered
scepter rod or wand that serves as a symbol of royal authority

An ancient god of fire in Roman mythology, Vulcan is the counterpart of the Greek god Hephaestus, the god of fire and **patron** of metalwork and crafts. The tales about Vulcan, who is sometimes called Mulciber (the smelter), are all based on Greek myths about Hephaestus.

The son of Zeus† and Hera† (or, in some versions, of Hera alone), Hephaestus was lame and deformed. Some stories say that Zeus threw him from Olympus† for taking Hera's side in a quarrel with Zeus and that Hephaestus became lame as a result of the fall. Other myths say that Hephaestus was born lame and that Hera threw him from Olympus because she was ashamed of his deformity. He landed in the ocean and was rescued by sea **nymphs,** who raised him in a cave under the sea and taught him many skills.

Hephaestus became a master craftsman. One day he gained his revenge on Hera by creating for her a golden throne that contained a trap. When she sat on the throne, the trap closed and imprisoned her. The other gods begged Hephaestus to release Hera, but he would not listen. Finally, the god Dionysus† made Hephaestus drunk and obtained the key to the trap.

As craftsman for the gods, Hephaestus built palaces and other beautiful and wondrous things that enabled the Olympians to live in great luxury. He also fashioned thunderbolts for Zeus, armor for the heroes Achilles† and Aeneas† that made them **invincible,** and a **scepter** for King Agamemnon† that gave him great power. Some legends say that Hephaestus created Pandora so that Zeus could take revenge on Prometheus† for giving fire to humans. Hephaestus later made the chains that bound Prometheus to a mountain.

Hephaestus often appeared as a comic figure in myths and had little luck in love. One time he took an ax and split Zeus's skull to

relieve a headache, and the goddess Athena† sprang fully grown from the head. He fell in love with Athena, but she rejected him. He also courted Aphrodite†, who accepted his offer of marriage but then had love affairs with others, including the god Ares†. Hephaestus fashioned a fine golden net and caught his wife and Ares in it. He then called the other gods so that they could laugh at the couple, but instead they mocked Hephaestus. The gods often made fun of him because of his limp and his soot-covered face, which came from working over the fire at his craft.

The Greeks believed that Hephaestus had a workshop on the volcanic island of Lemnos in the Aegean Sea. There, he taught the people the arts of metalwork, for which they became famous. The Romans thought that their god Vulcan lived and worked under Mount Etna, a volcano on the island of Sicily, and had workshops on Olympus and beneath other volcanoes as well. Each year in August, the Romans held a festival in honor of Vulcan called the Vulcanalia. **See also** ACHILLES; AENEAS; APHRODITE; ATHENA; FIRE; GREEK MYTHOLOGY; HERA; PANDORA; PROMETHEUS; ROMAN MYTHOLOGY; ZEUS.

Wakan Tanka

In Native American mythology, Wakan Tanka (great mystery) is the supreme being and creator of the Lakota Sioux. Sometimes called Great Spirit, he is similar to the supreme beings found in the myths of many other North American peoples.

According to Lakota myth, before creation Wakan Tanka existed in a great emptiness called Han (darkness). Feeling lonely, he decided to create companions for himself. First, Great Spirit focused his energy into a powerful force to form Inyan (rock), the first god. Next, he used Inyan to create Maka (earth) and then mated with that god to produce Skan (sky). Skan brought forth Wi (the sun) from Inyan, Maka, and himself. These four gods were separate and powerful, but they were all part of Wakan Tanka.

The first four gods produced four companions—Moon, Wind, Falling Star, and Thunderbird—to help with the process of creation. In turn, these companions created various gods and spirits, including Whirlwind, Four Winds, Buffalo, Two-Legged Creatures (humans and bears), Sicun (thought), Nagi (spirit of death), Niya (breath of life), and Nagila (shadow). All of these beings were aspects of Wakan Tanka. Together, they created and oversee everything that exists. **See also** CREATION STORIES; NATIVE AMERICAN MYTHOLOGY.

Wandjina

In Australian mythology, the Wandjina are ancestral beings who came out of the sea. According to the Aborigines of the western Kimberleys region, these beings created features of the landscape and were then absorbed into the walls of rock formations.

Legends about the Wandjina say that they once caused a great flood that devastated the landscape and wiped out the human race. Disappointed with the corrupt behavior of humans, the Wandjina opened their mouths and released a torrent of water.

†*See **Names and Places** at the end of this volume for further information.*

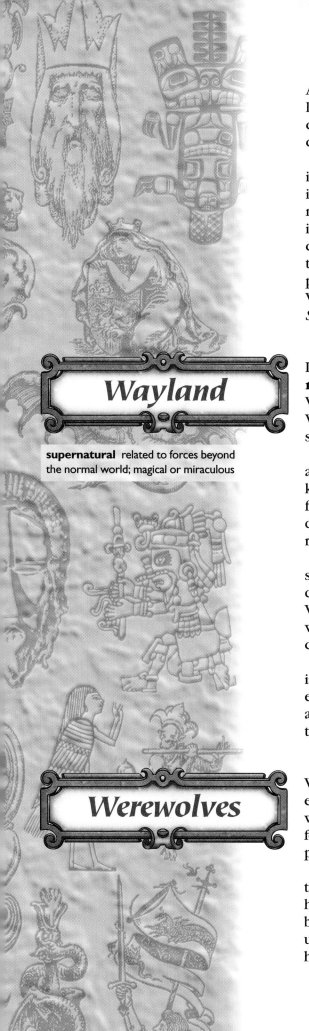

After the flood, the Wandjina spread out to different parts of the land. They created new humans and helped them set up a new society. To prevent further floods, the Wandjina kept their mouths closed. In time, their mouths disappeared completely.

Images of the Wandjina in human form appear in rock paintings in northwestern Australia. The figures have round faces, painted in white, with eyes and noses but no mouths. The heads are surrounded by a band of yellow or red, and white stripes on the bodies represent the falling rain. Each year during a cycle of religious ceremonies, the Aborigines repaint the figures to bring fertility to the land and ensure that the seasons change on schedule. By repainting these images from the past, the Aborigines make the Wandjina part of the present and preserve them for the future. ***See also*** AUSTRALIAN MYTHOLOGY; CREATION STORIES; DREAMTIME.

Wayland

supernatural related to forces beyond the normal world; magical or miraculous

In myths from northern Europe, a legendary smith used **supernatural** skills to make weapons and magical items. Known as Wayland in England, the smith appears in Norse† mythology as Volund and in German mythology as Wieland. According to some stories, he was lord of the elves.

The son of a giant and grandson of a mermaid, Wayland served as an apprentice to the wise craftsman Mimir. King Nidud, an evil king of Sweden, captured Wayland and forced the smith to work for him. To prevent Wayland from escaping, the king cut the tendons in his feet, making him lame. He also placed the smith on a remote island.

Wayland took revenge on King Nidud by killing his two young sons and raping his daughter. He crafted gold and jewel-studded drinking bowls from the boys' skulls and sent them to the king. Wayland escaped his island prison by flying away on magical wings (or in some versions a feathered robe), which he had crafted for himself.

English tradition associates Wayland with an ancient stone burial chamber in southern England known as Wayland's Smithy. Legend says that if a traveler ties a horse there, leaves some money, and goes away for a while, horseshoes will appear magically on the animal's hooves. ***See also*** NORSE MYTHOLOGY.

Werewolves

Werewolves are man-wolves—*wer* is Old English for "man." Legends from around the world tell of men who could turn into wolves and then back into human form again. In their animal form, werewolves were bloodthirsty creatures that devoured people, both living and dead.

Legends of people changing into animals occur in all parts of the world. In countries where wolves are unknown, such legends have involved tigers, leopards, hyenas, bears, panthers, snakes, boars, and other animals. Perhaps these stories reflect a universal unease about the more bestial aspects of human nature and behavior. Some scholars have suggested that these transformation

95

deity god or goddess

legends are faint echoes of ancient ceremonies in which people wore animal skins and masks.

European werewolf tales date from ancient times. Among other stories, Ovid† wrote that a Greek king named Lycaon was turned into a wolf as punishment for serving human flesh to the gods. From the Greek words *lukos* (wolf) and *anthropos* (man) comes *lycanthropy,* which refers to the werewolf's transformation. Modern psychologists also use the term to describe a mental illness in which the patient believes he or she is a wolf or some other animal.

Belief in werewolves was widespread in Europe during the Middle Ages. Any infant born with body hair, a strange birthmark, or a caul (a membrane covering the head) was thought to be a potential werewolf. It was believed that a person could become a werewolf voluntarily, generally by embracing black magic or worshiping the devil. The bite of a werewolf could also turn someone into a werewolf.

One of the most frightening aspects of werewolf legends was the idea that the cannibalistic beast could pass his days as a mild and righteous citizen, unsuspected of any evil. In some traditions, the werewolf took on animal form at will, perhaps every night. Other traditions, however, said that the transformation occurred only on nights of the full moon.

Folktales offered various tips about how to injure or kill a werewolf. Some suggested that any weapon that could hurt an ordinary wolf could harm a werewolf as well and that when the beast returned to its human form, its injuries would reveal its identity as a werewolf. Other legends said that only special weapons made of silver or possessing religious powers or blessings could harm a werewolf. ***See also*** ANIMALS IN MYTHOLOGY; MONSTERS; VAMPIRES.

White Shell Woman

White Shell Woman appears in the creation stories of various Native American tribes, including the Navajo, Zuni, and Apache. In Zuni myth, White Shell Woman is an ancestor of the Sun Father, a creator god and the source of life. She lives with him in the West.

In the Navajo creation story, White Shell Woman (Yoolgai asdzáá) is the sister of the goddess Changing Woman and a wife of Water. Created when the Talking God and the Wind breathed life into two shells, the sisters grew lonely and sought company—Changing Woman with the Sun and White Shell Woman with a mountain stream. Eventually they gave birth to two sons, who grew up to battle the monsters that roamed the earth. In some Navajo tales, White Shell Woman and Changing Woman become the same character.

According to the Navajo, when White Shell Woman went to live on her own, the Talking God and other **deities** came to visit her. They brought ears of corn that they covered with sacred blankets to create a man and a woman. White Shell Woman was overjoyed with this couple, who along with the descendants of Changing Woman became the ancestors of the Navajo people. ***See also*** CHANGING WOMAN; CREATION STORIES; NATIVE AMERICAN MYTHOLOGY.

†*See **Names and Places** at the end of this volume for further information.*

Whittington, Dick

Both a legendary and historical figure, Dick Whittington was an English merchant and Lord Mayor of London. The real Dick Whittington was the son of a knight, and he became rich and famous selling fabrics to kings and nobles. The wealthiest merchant of his day, he served three terms as Lord Mayor of London in the late 1300s and early 1400s.

English legend, however, places Dick Whittington as a poor orphan boy from the countryside who went to London because he had heard that the city streets were paved with silver and gold. In search of a job, he found work as a cook's helper in the home of a wealthy merchant. The cook treated Dick very badly, so he ran away. On his way out of the city, however, he heard church bells ringing. They seemed to say "Turn again, Whittington, Lord Mayor of great London," so he stopped and returned to the city.

Upon reaching his master's house, Whittington discovered that his only possession, a cat, had been sold for a huge sum to a Moorish ruler of North Africa, whose kingdom was overrun with rats. Whittington invested the money wisely and became a successful and rich merchant. He married his master's daughter and became Lord Mayor of London.

Witches and Wizards

supernatural related to forces beyond the normal world; magical or miraculous

Witches and wizards are people thought to possess magical powers or to command **supernatural** forces. They appear in the myths and folktales of many cultures. The word *witch* usually refers to a female, though male witches exist in some traditions. Men who possess the powers associated with witchcraft are often known as wizards or warlocks.

Bad or Good? In many myths and legends, witches are evil, dishonest, or dangerous. Some cultures do not consider them fully human. If not evil by nature, witches may be possessed by demons or wicked spirits determined to harm humans. Yet ordinary men and women may learn magic for the purpose of hurting others. Such people are sometimes called sorcerers and sorceresses rather than wizards and witches. African tradition distinguishes between good magicians, or medicine men, and bad magicians, or sorcerers. Both types are distinct from the nonhuman witch.

During the Middle Ages in Europe, the belief in witches was widespread. Witches were said to be worshipers of the Devil. Thousands of women and some men were tortured and executed after being accused of witchcraft. The English who settled in North America brought along a fear of witches. A witch hunt in Salem, Massachusetts, in 1692 resulted in the execution of 19 people. Even today, accusations of witchcraft can lead to violence in some parts of the world.

Not all witches and wizards are evil. Some myths and folktales feature good spirits or magicians who help people. These are said to practice "white magic" rather than the "black magic" of the evil witches and wizards. *The Wonderful Wizard of Oz,* the modern

Arthurian legends identify Morgan Le Fay as the enchantress known as Nimuë, or the Lady of the Lake. In this role, she tricks Arthur's magician Merlin into falling in love with her. After learning Merlin's secrets, she imprisons him behind invisible walls.

children's book that became a famous movie, features both kinds of witches. It is easy to tell them apart—the wicked witch is an old, cackling hag dressed in black; the good witch is a beautiful, soft-spoken woman dressed like a princess.

The magicians that appear in myths and folktales, however, are not always clearly labeled. They may be unpredictable and of uncertain character—neither completely good nor completely evil. Their treatment of humans may depend on how they are treated. Often people meet old women, not realizing that they are dealing with witches. In such cases, the witch may reward kindness and punish rudeness.

Legendary Witches and Wizards. Witches take many forms. The traditional image in European and American folklore is that of a wrinkled old woman, perhaps wearing a black robe and a cone-shaped hat. These witches communicate with evil spirits called familiars, which often take the form of a black cat. According to legend, Japanese witches have owls as familiars, and African witches have monkeys.

Flight is often associated with witchcraft. In American folktales, witches usually travel through the night skies on enchanted

† *See **Names and Places** at the end of this volume for further information.*

A Wizard's Education

Stories about witches and wizards continue to fascinate the public and to inspire writers. In addition to providing an otherworldly atmosphere, such stories often reveal truths about ordinary human existence. In the series of modern fantasy books about Harry Potter, the Scottish writer J. K. Rowling describes an entire society involved with magic. The reader follows Harry, an ordinary boy, as he studies at the Hogwarts School for Witchcraft and Wizardry. Between adventures laced with dragons, magic potions, and flying broomsticks, Rowling shows how Harry learns about values such as friendship, loyalty, and courage.

broomsticks. In some parts of Africa, witches are said to fly on bats. African witches often take the form of animals and eat human flesh. In the mythology of some cultures, witches can change into animals to prey upon their victims.

The tradition of witchcraft is ancient. The book of Samuel in the Old Testament of the Bible contains an account of a sorceress called the Witch of Endor. Saul, the first king of Israel, banished magicians from his kingdom but finally asked for advice from the Witch of Endor, who had "a familiar spirit." Assured that she would not be punished for practicing magic, the witch called up the spirit of Samuel, a dead prophet of the Israelites. The spirit predicted Saul's defeat in the battle that was to take place the next day.

In the *Odyssey*†, an **epic** of ancient Greece, the hero Odysseus† and his men met a witch named Circe. The daughter of a god and an ocean **nymph**, Circe had the power to turn people into animals and monsters. Her island home was populated with lions, bears, and wolves—humans who had been transformed by her magic. Although she turned some of Odysseus's men into pigs, the hero used a special herb that protected him from her magic.

Witchcraft and magic played an important role in the Arthurian legends† of Britain. Merlin, a powerful wizard, guided and influenced King Arthur throughout his life. A witch named Morgan Le Fay also appeared in the legends and took care of Arthur after he was wounded in battle.

Slavic folklore of eastern Europe and western Russia has a witch called Baba Yaga, a thin old woman whose nickname means bony legs. Baba Yaga lives alone in a hut deep in the forest. The hut stands on the legs of a chicken and is surrounded by a fence decorated with skulls. Visitors who wish to enter must recite a magic formula. Although Baba Yaga sometimes helps the hero or heroine of a story, she is generally a dangerous figure who must be outwitted.

One Baba Yaga story concerns a prince named Ivan, who needed a very fast horse to rescue his wife from the clutches of a monster. Ivan learned that Baba Yaga had some special horses and asked her for the use of one. The witch said that he must first guard her horses for three nights. She was sure that Ivan would fail at the task because she ordered the horses to gallop away each night. However, Ivan had shown kindness to various animals and insects, and they gathered the horses together for him. Finally Ivan seized one of the horses and rode off to save his wife. Baba Yaga chased him, but he outran her.

Witches and sorcerers occur frequently in Native American myths. Unlike **shamans** and healers, they are fearsome and destructive beings. The Navajo of the American Southwest have stories about the *adilgashii*, witches who travel at night in the skins of coyotes or other animals and who use poison made from the ground-up bones of babies to harm the living. In English, the *adilgashii* are called skinwalkers.

The Tlingit of the Pacific Northwest believe that a man with an unfaithful wife becomes a witch by drinking from a dead shaman's skull. This first witch then creates other witches, both male and

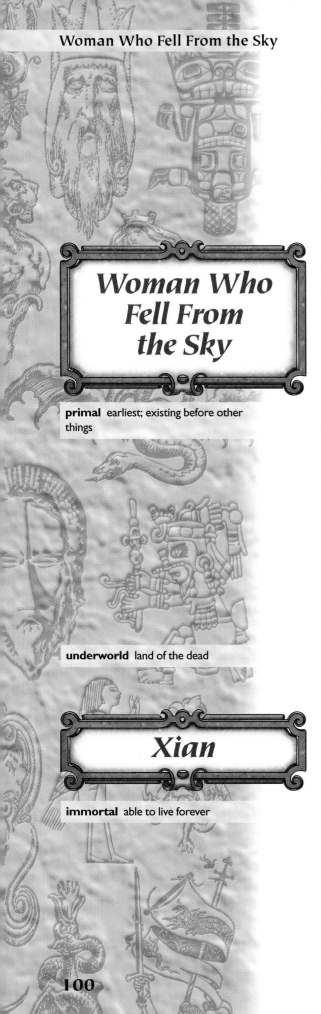

Woman Who Fell From the Sky

primal earliest; existing before other things

underworld land of the dead

Xian

immortal able to live forever

female. They acquire dark powers by lurking in graveyards and handling the dead. In a theme repeated in stories from many cultures, the Tlingit witches make dolls out of the hair, clothing, or food of those they want to harm. By placing these dolls in graves to rot with corpses, the witches cause their victims to become sick. A witch can reverse the spell and cure the victim by rinsing the doll in salt water. *See also* CIRCE; DEVILS AND DEMONS; MERLIN; MONSTERS; MORGAN LE FAY.

In the mythology of the Iroquois and Huron of North America, the Woman Who Fell From the Sky is a **primal** ancestor. Also known as Sky Woman or Ataensic, she plays a central role in creation.

According to legend, the Woman Who Fell From the Sky lived in a world above the sky. One day she became pregnant and fell out of heaven. Some stories say that she fell while chasing a bear, while others say that the tree of life was uprooted and she tumbled through the hole left behind.

As the woman fell, ducks flew beneath her to slow her descent. She landed in a vast watery place, with no land in sight. Turtle arose from the water and let her rest on his back. Meanwhile, Muskrat dove beneath the water and brought up mud to form the earth. Soon after, the woman gave birth to twin sons—one good and one evil—who created all the natural features of the earth and sky. According to some stories, she gave birth to a daughter, and that woman was the mother of the twins.

The good twin shaped the sky and created the sun. He also made the moon, stars, mountains, and many plants and animals. The evil twin set out to destroy his brother's creations. He created darkness to drive the sun from the sky and made monsters, storms, and various kinds of dangerous beasts. When creation was finished, the brothers fought. The good twin won and banished his evil brother from the earth. Some stories say that the evil twin became ruler of the **underworld** and still tries to spread evil in the world. *See also* CREATION STORIES; NATIVE AMERICAN MYTHOLOGY; TWINS.

In the Taoist mythology of China, the Xian (or Hsien) are a group of eight **immortal** characters who at one time lived as humans on earth. Some of the Xian were real individuals mentioned in historical records; others appear only in myths and legends.

Popular subjects in Chinese mythology and art, the Xian are said to travel the universe together in a state of perfect health and happiness. They perform various wonders and miracles and serve as models for those seeking the tao, or way—the path to an ideal state of being and existence. In Chinese art, these Eight Immortals often appear as a group, each depicted with his or her own characteristic clothing and possessions.

How the Xian Achieved Immortality. The stories about the Xian explain how each achieved immortality in a different way.

The first to reach this state was Li Tieguai (Iron Crutch), a hermit who went 40 years without food or sleep. According to some stories, Li Tieguai acquired immortality and his crutch from the Queen Mother of the West, who saw him limping and begging. Other legends say that Laozi, the founder of Taoism, came down from heaven to teach Li Tieguai the wisdom of the gods. One day Li sent his spirit to Laozi. When he returned, he found that a follower had burned his body, believing him to be dead. So Li entered the body of a deformed beggar who had died, gaining both immortality and a new identity.

Several different tales tell of the life of Han Zhongli, an army officer and state official. Some stories say that after losing a battle he went into the mountains, became a hermit, and learned the secret of immortality from the Flowers of the East. Other tales say that he was a priest or a beggar and that he discovered a jade box containing the magic potion of eternal life. In art, Han Zhongli is usually portrayed as a bearded old man holding a fan made of feathers.

Lu Dongbin. The most famous of the Xian was Lu Dongbin, a prince who traveled throughout China slaying dragons with a magic sword. One day he met Han Zhongli at an inn, and later that night he dreamed that his royal life would end in disgrace. When he awoke, he turned his back on worldly things and followed Han Zhongli into the mountains to seek the tao and gain immortality. Lu Dongbin is usually shown carrying a sword.

The grandnephew of a great statesman and poet, Han Xiang became a follower of Lu Dongbin. While climbing a sacred peach tree one day, he fell from the branches and achieved immortality before he reached the ground. Some stories say he died as a result of the fall and was then transformed into an immortal. Han Xiang is shown in art carrying a basket of flowers.

Cao Guojiu was the brother of an empress. Disgusted by the corruption at the royal court, he went into the mountains to seek the tao. He met a boatman on the way and showed him a golden tablet that would admit the holder to the royal court. The boatman—Lu Dongbin in disguise—was not impressed, but he took Cao Guojiu as a disciple and taught him the tao and the secret of immortality. In art, Cao Guojiu appears wearing official robes and carrying his golden tablet.

The immortal Zhang Guolao was also a hermit. Famous for his skills in magic, he traveled around on a white mule that he could fold up like a sheet of paper and put into a carrying bag. Many stories say that

In the Taoist mythology of China, the Xian are a group of eight immortal characters who travel the universe together in a state of perfect health and happiness. The Eight Immortals are often seen in a group; they appear here in a boat crossing the sea.

underworld land of the dead

Xibalba

Zhang Guolao achieved immortality simply by never dying or by appearing alive again after people saw him die. In art he is shown with a peach—a symbol of immortality—and a feather from the legendary phoenix.

The immortal Lan Caihe sometimes appears as a man and other times as a woman. One day while gathering medicinal herbs, Lan Caihe met a beggar and helped tend the sores on his body. The beggar was Li Tieguai in disguise, and he rewarded this kindness by granting Lan Caihe immortality. Lan Caihe traveled around the country in a tattered blue dress, urging people to seek the tao. He is usually shown with a flute or a basket of fruit.

The eighth Xian, He Xiangu, is the only one who is definitely a woman. As a young girl, He Xiangu dreamed that a spirit told her to grind up and eat some mother-of-pearl. She did this and became immortal. Thereafter, she floated from mountain to mountain gathering herbs and fruit. Artists generally portrayed her as a beautiful woman wearing a lotus flower in her hair or on her clothing.

The Qi Xian. The Eight Immortals were also known as the Ba Xian, a title that distinguished them from the Qi Xian, a group of seven Chinese poets and scholars who lived in the A.D. 200s. The Qi Xian, known as the Seven Sages of the Bamboo Grove, were historical figures who retreated to the countryside to write works that embraced Taoist ideas and that criticized the corruption of the royal court. Their self-imposed exile served as a model for later Chinese writers seeking to escape worldly troubles. *See also* CHINESE MYTHOLOGY.

In the mythology of the Maya of Middle America, Xibalba (place of fright) was an underground realm of the dead. Caves and pools of water served as entry points to the realm. During the later part of its history, the Mayan empire was sometimes called the empire of Xibalba.

A story recorded in the *Popol Vuh,* the sacred book of the Maya, tells of a visit to Xibalba by the Hero Twins, Hunahpú and Xbalanqúe. Much earlier their father and uncle, also twins, had been summoned by the powerful lords of Xibalba. Disturbed by the brothers' ball playing on earth, the lords had invited them to the **underworld** for a ball game and then killed them.

Later Hunahpú and Xbalanqúe were also ordered to come to Xibalba. There they passed through a series of trials in various houses, and in each house they faced a test of their wits, strength, and courage. In the Dark House, for example, they had to endure darkness. In the Razor House they "tamed" the blades that were supposed to kill them and persuaded the cutting ants to bring them flowers, which they presented to the lords of Xibalba.

The Hero Twins eventually tricked and killed the lords of Xibalba. The people of the underworld surrendered to the twins, who sentenced them to pass their time making pottery and other humble tools rather than playing ball. The Hero Twins escaped from the underworld through their cleverness and determination, setting an example that the souls of kings and nobles could try to follow. *See also* HUNAHPÚ AND XBALANQÚE; MAYAN MYTHOLOGY; POPOL VUH.

Xiuhtecuhtli

deity god or goddess
patron special guardian, protector, or supporter
cosmology set of ideas about the origin, history, and structure of the universe
underworld land of the dead

In the mythology of the Aztecs of central Mexico, Xiuhtecuhtli was a god of fire. A young and vigorous **deity,** he was regarded as a **patron** of kings and warriors. His name meant Turquoise Lord, and images of Xiuhtecuhtli often show him wearing a crown and ornaments made of that much-prized blue stone. Xiuhtecuhtli had another name—Huehueteotl, the Old God—and a different image. As Huehueteotl, he appeared as an elderly man, usually bent over and carrying a brazier, or small stove, on his head.

Xiuhtecuhtli played a vital role in the Aztec **cosmology.** According to myths, he rose from a hearth in Mictlan, the Aztec **underworld,** and passed through earth to the heavens as a pillar of fire. If that fire—which held the parts of the universe together—were to die, everything would fall apart. Because he linked all the realms of the universe together, Xiuhtecuhtli was thought to be the guide who led souls from this life to the afterlife.

Xiuhtecuhtli also served as the god of time and the calendar—the word *xihuitl,* related to his name, meant "year." Festivals in his honor were held twice a year, once in midsummer and once in midwinter. A much more significant ceremony took place every 52 years, at the end of a time-keeping cycle called the Calendar Round. On this occasion, the Aztecs put out every fire in their empire. The priests of Xiuhtecuhtli lit a new sacred fire to begin the new Calendar Round. From this fire all the other fires were relit, first in the temples and then in people's homes. *See also* AZTEC MYTHOLOGY; FIRE; HUEHUETEOTL.

Yellow Emperor

patron special guardian, protector, or supporter
culture hero mythical figure who gives people the tools of civilization, such as language and fire
benevolent desiring good for others

In Chinese mythology, Huang-Di (the Yellow Emperor) was the most ancient of five legendary Chinese emperors as well as a **patron** of Taoism, one of China's main religions and philosophies. He was also a **culture hero,** credited with civilizing the earth, teaching people many skills, and inventing numerous useful items, including the wheel, armor and weapons, ships, writing, the compass, and coined money.

According to tradition, the Yellow Emperor began ruling in 2697 B.C. His long reign was said to be a golden age, and he was honored as a **benevolent** and wise ruler. Before Huang-Di came to the throne, order and government were unknown in the world. He introduced systems of government and law to humankind, and he also invented music and the arts.

Legend says that the Yellow Emperor had four faces that gazed out in four directions, allowing him to see all that happened in the world. In addition, he could communicate directly with the gods through his prayers and sacrifices. When he traveled around his empire, he rode in an ivory chariot pulled by dragons and an elephant,

In Chinese mythology, Huang-Di was a legendary Chinese emperor and supporter of Taoism. A kind and wise ruler, he introduced systems of government, law, music, and art to China.

accompanied by a procession of tigers, wolves, snakes, and flocks of the fabled phoenix birds.

During Huang-Di's reign, only one god challenged his authority. The rebel god was aided by the emperor's son Fei Lian, lord of the wind. They sent fogs and rain to drown the **imperial** armies, but the emperor's daughter Ba (drought) dried up the rains and helped defeat the rebels.

After ruling for many years, Huang-Di became tired and weak. He allowed officials to make decisions for him and went to live in a simple hut in the courtyard of his palace. Through fasting, prayer, and meditation, he discovered the tao, or way—a belief that leads to an ideal state of being. The Yellow Emperor continued to rule for many additional years, attempting to bring a state of perfection to his realm. Upon his death he rose into the heavens and became a Xian (or Hsien), an **immortal.** *See also* CHINESE MYTHOLOGY; HEROES; XIAN.

imperial relating to an emperor or empire
immortal able to live forever

Yggdrasill

underworld land of the dead

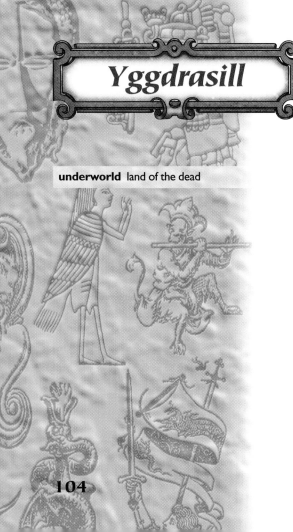

In Norse† mythology, a mighty axis, or pole, ran through the universe in which the gods, giants, and heroes enacted their stormy dramas. That axis, around which all life revolved, was the World Tree, a giant ash tree called Yggdrasill.

The myths paint a complex picture of how the universe was structured around Yggdrasill. Sometimes the World Tree is described as running through nine realms, from the shadowy depths of the **underworld** up to the heavenly abode of the gods. At other times, the trunk of Yggdrasill is said to anchor Midgard, the world of humans, while the tree's three great roots reach down into Jotunheim, the land of the frost giants; Niflheim, the land of mist; and Asgard, the home of the gods.

Although the World Tree offered an avenue of passage from one realm to the next, the distances and dangers involved in such travel were great. The only creature that could run up and down Yggdrasill easily was a squirrel, which carried insulting messages between a fierce eagle perched in the tree's topmost branch and a dragon that gnawed at its root. Yggdrasill existed in a state of delicate balance, being endlessly destroyed and renewed.

The World Tree was closely linked to sources of hidden or magical knowledge. Its name, which means "Odin's horse," refers to Odin† hanging himself from the tree for nine days and nights to learn secret mysteries. Near one root rose a spring whose waters provided wisdom. Odin was said to have traded an eye to drink

*† See **Names and Places** at the end of this volume for further information.*

this water. Another root sheltered a spring tended by the Norns, three women who determined the fate of all humans. ***See also*** **NORSE MYTHOLOGY; TREES IN MYTHOLOGY.**

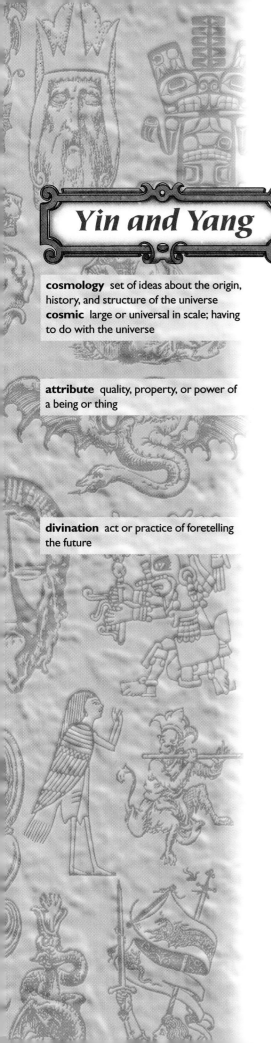

Yin and Yang

cosmology set of ideas about the origin, history, and structure of the universe
cosmic large or universal in scale; having to do with the universe

attribute quality, property, or power of a being or thing

divination act or practice of foretelling the future

Chinese mythology and **cosmology** rest on the idea that the universe is shaped and maintained by two fundamental forces called Yin and Yang. Although opposites, Yin and Yang are not in conflict with one another. Rather, they interact constantly, achieving a delicate balance. Nature and society depend on this balance for harmony. When Yin and Yang fall out of balance, disaster follows.

According to tradition, the idea of two opposing but intertwined **cosmic** forces developed before 2000 B.C. The ancient notion underlies both Taoism and Confucianism, two of the major strands of Chinese philosophy and religion. The Japanese adopted Yin and Yang, calling them In and Yo.

Yin and Yang are represented in pairs of **attributes** or things that are opposites or halves of a whole. Yin is associated with the earth, darkness, femaleness, cold, moisture, softness, and inactivity. Yang is linked with the sky, light, maleness, heat, dryness, and activity. Yin is a negative force; Yang is a positive one. Yin is represented by a broken line, Yang by an unbroken one. Various combinations of broken and unbroken lines in groups of three, called trigrams, form the basis of an ancient Chinese work known as the *I Ching,* which is used in **divination.**

Beyond Yin and Yang lies a single absolute or ultimate reality called the T'ai Chi, a force or power that gives existence to all

In Chinese mythology, Yin and Yang are two fundamental, connected but opposing, forces that influence nature and society. A circular symbol called the T'ai Chi represents the power beyond Yin and Yang that gives existence to all things.

105

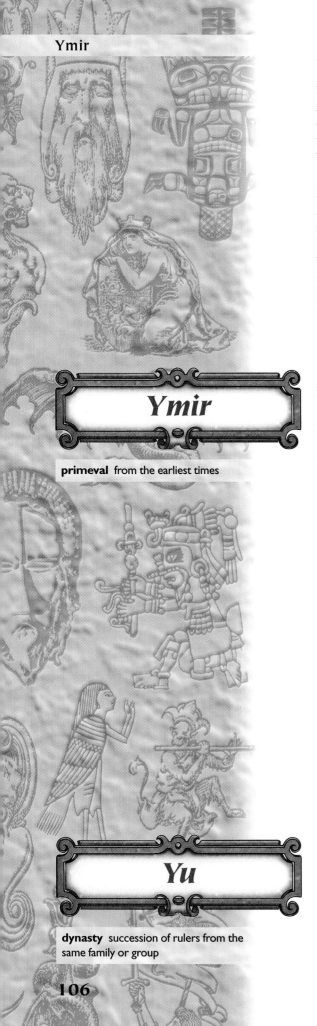

Yu's father, Kun, was placed in charge of keeping China's floods under control. After nine years of unsuccessful effort, Kun stole some magic soil from heaven to dam the waters. The theft angered the supreme god, who ordered Kun's execution. Three years later, Kun's miraculously preserved body was split open with a sword and Yu sprang forth.

Yu continued his father's work. According to some stories, he went to heaven and asked the supreme god for some earth, which he used to dam rivers and make channels. In other tales Yu discovered that the floods were caused by evil water monsters. He traveled the world, changing shape as necessary and battling the monsters. Meanwhile a winged dragon helped him drain the land by dragging its tail where channels were needed.

After 13 years of strenuous labor, Yu succeeded in controlling the floods. The channels he dug let water flow safely to the sea, and the drained marshlands became fit for farming. During all those years he never saw his wife and children, and he became worn out and lame from the hard labor. As a reward for his services, the ruler of China gave up the throne to Yu, who became the first emperor of the Hsia dynasty. According to Chinese tradition, Yu ruled from 2205 to 2197 B.C. *See also* CHINESE MYTHOLOGY; DRAGONS; FLOODS; HEROES.

Zeus

deity god or goddess

destiny future or fate of an individual or thing

patron special guardian, protector, or supporter

cult group bound together by devotion to a particular person, belief, or god

pantheon all the gods of a particular culture

cosmic large or universal in scale; having to do with the universe

Zeus was the most important **deity** of ancient Greece, the leader of the gods and the all-powerful overseer of earthly events and human **destiny**. His role in mythology was complex and filled with contradictions. Zeus was the god of law and social order, yet he came to power through violent revolution. A **patron** god of marriage and the household, he was repeatedly unfaithful to his own wife, Hera†, and fathered children by a variety of women.

As a mythological figure, Zeus changed over the centuries. Originally a sky god, he was believed to bring clouds, rain, thunder, and lightning. His **cults** were associated with mountain peaks where clouds gathered. As Greek mythology developed, the figure of Zeus grew larger until he became the dominant force in the Greek **pantheon**. Later, as Jupiter, he was the chief god of Rome.

The Father of Gods and Men. Some of the earliest accounts of Zeus appear in the writings of Homer† and Hesiod†. Homer called Zeus "the father of gods and men," but the term *father* referred more to Zeus's position of authority than to actual parenthood. Zeus did father some of the gods, but many others were his brothers and sisters, nephews, or nieces. Although he ruled many aspects of earthly affairs and human life, Zeus was not a creator god. Other mythological powers brought the earth and human beings into existence. Zeus enforced the **cosmic** laws that governed them.

In a myth that some modern scholars believe reflects the triumph of the Greek gods over more ancient deities, Hesiod told how Zeus became the supreme god. Before the gods existed, the

107

The leader of the Greek deities, Zeus was the god of law and social order. He also oversaw all earthly and divine events.

Titans ruled the universe. Their chief was Cronus†. He and his wife Rhea had five children, but because Cronus had been warned that one of his children would overthrow him, he devoured each child as soon as it was born. Zeus was the sixth. Rhea was determined to save this child, so she deceived Cronus by giving him a blanket-wrapped stone to swallow and secretly sent the infant to safety on the island of Crete. There, **nymphs** tended the baby Zeus, while Cretan warriors sang and clashed their swords so that Cronus would not hear his crying.

When he grew up, Zeus was ready to overthrow his cruel father and avenge the siblings that Cronus had swallowed. He befriended Metis, who was either a Titaness or an ocean nymph. Metis devised a potion to make Cronus vomit up his children, and either she or Zeus gave it to Cronus to drink. Cronus spat forth Zeus's sisters Hestia, Demeter†, and Hera and his brothers Hades† and Poseidon†. Last of all, Cronus vomited up the stone he had swallowed in place of Zeus. Tradition says that the stone was later set in a place of honor at Delphi†. It was called the *omphalos*, the navel of the world.

Zeus, Hades, and Poseidon battled the Titans in a conflict that lasted ten years. Zeus also had the help of 300 armed giants and of the Cyclopes, one-eyed giants imprisoned in Tartarus, a deep pit

*†See **Names and Places** at the end of this volume for further information.*

underworld land of the dead

demigod one who is part human and part god

Images of the God

Ancient artists generally depicted Zeus as a dignified, bearded man of middle age. Often, he was shown holding, or preparing to hurl, a thunderbolt, which took the form of a winged spear or a cylinder with pointed ends. One of the most remarkable images ever created of Zeus was a statue that stood in his temple at Olympia in Greece. The statue was lost long ago, but a description of it survives. The 40-foot-tall statue showed the god seated, with golden lions at his side. The head and upper body were made of precious ivory, and the lower body was draped in gold—truly a glorious and awe-inspiring representation of "the greatest god of all."

of the **underworld.** Released by Zeus, the Cyclopes forged a thunderbolt for him to use as a weapon. In the end, the Titans were overthrown, and Zeus sent all those who had opposed him to Tartarus. Only Atlas†, a Titan who had not fought against Zeus, was spared.

Zeus and his brothers divided the world. Zeus controlled the sky, Hades the underworld, and Poseidon the sea—although Zeus had ultimate control over his brothers. The gods and their sisters took up residence on Mount Olympus†, which is why they and their offspring are called the Olympian deities.

The Loves of Zeus. Zeus fathered children with a series of partners—nymphs, Titanesses, goddesses, and mortal women. The offspring of these unions included deities, **demigods,** and heroes.

Accounts of Zeus's loves and children vary somewhat, but Metis is usually listed as his first partner or wife. When she became pregnant, Zeus learned that her child would be a powerful god who would one day replace him. Like his father Cronus before him, Zeus was determined to preserve his power, but he did not wait to swallow the infant—he swallowed Metis. Their child, Athena†, emerged full-grown from Zeus's head.

Next, Zeus turned to the Titaness Themis, who bore him two sets of daughters known as the Fates and the Hours. The ocean nymph Eurynome also had daughters by Zeus, including the Graces. His next wife or partner was his sister, the goddess Demeter. (Marriages between brother and sister deities occur in the mythologies of many ancient cultures.) Their child, Persephone, later became the wife of Hades.

Zeus's union with the Titaness Mnemosyne (memory) produced the nine goddesses known as the Muses. Leto bore Zeus's twins Apollo† and Artemis†. Maia, the daughter of Atlas, bore him Hermes†. Eventually, Zeus married Hera, his last wife and the mother of three more Olympian deities: Ares†, Hebe, and Hephaestus† (Vulcan).

Yet Zeus continued to have love affairs, many of them with mortal women. He sometimes mated with them in disguise or in animal form. After he visited the princess Danaë as a shower of gold, she bore Perseus†. To Europa, another princess, he appeared as a white bull. He came to Leda in the form of a swan. The children of their union were Helen of Troy, her sister Clytemnestra, and the brothers Castor and Pollux. His most famous half-human son was Hercules†, born to Alcmena, to whom he came disguised as her own husband.

Zeus's relations with other women infuriated Hera, and she despised all the children he fathered by these women. Hera particularly hated Hercules and frequently tried to harm him. Once, when she had gone too far, Zeus hanged her in the heavens with a heavy block pulling her feet down, and he threw Hephaestus out of Olympus for trying to help her.

Surviving Hera's attacks, Hercules aided Zeus and the other Olympians in a battle for survival. They were challenged by a race

109

of giants, which Gaia, the earth, had produced to bring an end to their rule. Zeus defeated the giants as well as various other threats to his supremacy, including a conspiracy among Hera, Athena, and Poseidon.

The Roman Jupiter. The Romans, who adopted many elements of Greek culture and mythology, came to identify their own sky god, Jupiter, with Zeus. Associated with weather and agriculture in early Roman myths, Jupiter was the patron god of storms, thunder, lightning, the sowing of seeds, and the harvesting of grapes. As Roman civilization developed, Jupiter became known as Optimus Maximus, which means "best and greatest." He was viewed as the supreme god and the protector of the Roman state. As Rome became a military power, Jupiter took on such titles as "supreme commander," "unconquerable," and "triumphant."

Although Jupiter acquired many of the characteristics and myths associated with Zeus, his marriage to the goddess Juno was more harmonious than that of Zeus and Hera. Moreover, Jupiter shared some of his power with Juno and the goddess Minerva (the Roman version of Athena). The three deities were believed to preside jointly over both divine and earthly affairs. ***See also*** ATHENA; ATLAS; CASTOR AND POLLUX; CRONUS; CYCLOPES; DANAË; DEMETER; GAIA; GRACES; GREEK MYTHOLOGY; HADES; HELEN OF TROY; HERA; HERCULES; MUSES; PERSEPHONE; POSEIDON; ROMAN MYTHOLOGY; TITANS; VULCAN.

Zoroastrian Mythology

See ***Persian Mythology.***

Glossary

A

abbot head of a monastery or abbey

abduction carrying away by force

abyss very deep gulf or hole

adultery sexual relationship between a married person and someone other than his or her spouse

adversary enemy; opponent

allegory literary and artistic device in which characters represent an idea or a religious or moral principle

allot to assign a portion or share

amulet small object thought to have supernatural or magical powers

ankh cross with a loop at the top; Egyptian symbol of life

anoint to bless by applying oil or some other substance

anti-Semitism prejudice against Jews

apocalypse prediction of a sudden and violent end of the world

archaeological referring to the study of past human cultures, usually by excavating ruins

aristocracy privileged upper classes of society; nobles or the nobility

artisan skilled crafts worker

attribute quality, property, or power of a being or thing

B

ballad popular song, often telling a story

barbarism savage or primitive state

benevolent desiring good for others

booty riches or property gained through conquest

C

cabalistic referring to a system of mystical thought based on a secret interpretation of the Hebrew Scriptures

caste division of people in Hindu society into classes based on birth

catacombs underground tunnels near Rome used as hiding and gathering places for early Christians

cauldron large kettle

centaur half-human, half-animal creature with the body of a horse and the head, chest, and arms of a human

chalice drinking vessel or goblet

chameleon lizard that can change color

chaos great disorder or confusion

chastity purity or virginity

cherubim winged lions; in later times, angels portrayed as winged human figures

chivalry rules and customs of medieval knighthood

city-state independent state consisting of a city and its surrounding territory

clan group of people descended from a common ancestor or united by a common interest

clay tablet baked clay slab inscribed with ancient writings

conquistador Spanish military explorer and conqueror

cosmic large or universal in scale; having to do with the universe

cosmology set of ideas about the origin, history, and structure of the universe

cosmos the universe, especially as an orderly and harmonious system

cult group bound together by devotion to a particular person, belief, or god

culture hero mythical figure who gives people the tools of civilization, such as language and fire

D

deify to make a god or goddess

deity god or goddess

demigod one who is part human and part god

destiny future or fate of an individual or thing

differentiation process of becoming different and separate from another thing

discord disagreement

discus heavy, circular plate hurled over distance as a sport

divination act or practice of foretelling the future

doctrine set of principles or beliefs accepted by a group

dowry money, goods, or property that a woman brings to her husband at marriage

dualistic consisting of two equal and opposing forces

dynasty succession of rulers from the same family or group

E

embalm to treat a corpse with oils or chemicals to prevent or slow down the process of decay

enlightenment in Buddhism, a spiritual state marked by the absence of desire and suffering

epic long poem about legendary or historical heroes, written in a grand style

F

flail tool for threshing grain

floral having to do with flowers

G

genealogy record of a person's ancestry

genie spirit that serves the person who summons it

gluttony excessive eating or drinking

Gorgon one of three ugly monsters who had snakes for hair, staring eyes, and huge wings

H

Hellenistic term referring to the Greek-influenced culture of the Mediterranean world and the Near East during the three centuries after the death of Alexander the Great in 323 B.C.

heraldry practice of tracing family history and determining family emblems

hereditary passed on from parent to child

heretic person whose beliefs are contrary to church doctrine

hierarchy organization of a group into higher and lower levels

hieroglyphics ancient system of writing based on pictorial characters

Holy Grail sacred cup said to have been used by Jesus Christ at the Last Supper

hubris excessive pride or self-confidence

I

imminent about to take place; threatening

immortal able to live forever

immortality ability to live forever

imperial relating to an emperor or empire

incantation chant, often part of a magical formula or spell

incarnation appearance of a god, spirit, or soul in earthly form

indigenous native to a certain place

inundation floodwaters that cover the land

invincible too powerful to be conquered

invulnerable incapable of being hurt

Islam religion based on the teachings of the prophet Muhammad; religious faith of Muslims

J

jackal small, doglike mammal native to Asia and Africa

joust fight on horseback between two knights

L

lunar relating to the moon

lust strong desire

lyre stringed instrument similar to a small harp

M

maize corn

malevolent doing or wishing harm or ill toward others

manipulate to influence or control in a clever or underhanded way

martial having to do with warfare

martyr person who suffers or is put to death for a belief

matriarchal describing a society in which women hold the dominant positions

mediator go-between

medieval relating to the Middle Ages in Europe, a period from about A.D. 500 to 1500

meditate to think

Mesoamerica cultural region consisting of southern Mexico and northern regions of Central America

monotheism belief in only one god

monotheistic believing in only one god

Moors Spanish Muslims descended from the Arab conquerors

morality ideas about what is right and wrong in human conduct

mortuary having to do with the burial of the dead

mosaic picture made up of many small colored stones or tiles

mummification preservation of a body by removing its organs and allowing it to dry

mummify to preserve a body by removing its organs and allowing it to dry

Muse one of nine sister goddesses who presided over the arts and sciences

N

nymph minor goddess of nature, usually represented as young and beautiful

O

ogre hideous monster

omen sign of future events

oracle priest or priestess or other creature through whom a god is believed to speak; also the location (such as a shrine) where such words are spoken

P

pagan term used by early Christians to describe non-Christians and non-Christian beliefs

pantheon all the gods of a particular culture

papyrus writing material made by pressing together thin strips of the stem of the papyrus plant

patriarch man who is the founder or oldest member of a group

patriarchal describing a society in which men hold the dominant positions

patrician aristocrat or member of the noble class

patron special guardian, protector, or supporter

persecute to harass or punish individuals or groups

personification presenting in human form or with human qualities

pharaoh ruler of ancient Egypt

piety faithfulness to beliefs

pious faithful to one's beliefs

predetermined decided in advance

primal earliest; existing before other things

primeval from the earliest times

prophecy foretelling of what is to come; also something that is predicted

prophet one who claims to have received divine messages or insights

prose language that is not in poetic form

pyre pile of wood on which a dead body is burned in a funeral ceremony

R

relics pieces of bone, possessions, or other items belonging to a saint or sacred person

Renaissance artistic and intellectual movement that spread across Europe from the late 1300s through the 1500s

resurrect to raise from the dead

resurrection coming to life again; rising from the dead

revelation communication of divine truth or divine will

rite ceremony or formal procedure

ritual ceremony that follows a set pattern

romance in medieval literature, a tale based on legend, love, and adventure, often set in a distant place or time

S

saga story recounting the adventures of historical and legendary heroes; usually associated with Icelandic or Norse tales of the Middle Ages

satyr woodland deity that was part man and part goat or horse

scepter rod or wand that serves as a symbol of royal authority

scribe secretary or writer

sect religious group

seer one who can predict the future

serf peasant bound to a lord and required to work the lord's land

shaman person thought to possess spiritual and healing powers

siege attempt to conquer a city or fortress by surrounding it with troops and cutting off supplies

solar relating to the sun

soothsayer one who foretells events

sorcerer magician or wizard

steppe vast expanse of treeless grassland

subterranean under the earth

sultan ruler of a Persian or an Arabic state

supernatural related to forces beyond the normal world; magical or miraculous

T

taboo prohibition against doing something that is believed to cause harm

theology study of religious faith

Titan one of a family of giants who ruled the earth until overthrown by the Greek gods of Olympus

triad group of three

tribute payment made by a smaller or weaker party to a more powerful one, often under the threat of force

trickster mischievous figure appearing in various forms in the folktales and mythology of many different peoples

trident three-pronged spear, similar to a pitchfork

tsar Russian ruler

tyrant ruler (or other person) who uses power harshly or cruelly

U

underworld land of the dead

V

vassal individual who swears loyalty and obedience to a superior lord

Vestal Virgin priestess of the Roman goddess Vesta who was required to remain a virgin

W

winnow to separate the chaff, or useless part, of grain from the part that can be used for making flour

Names and Places

Achilles foremost warrior in Greek mythology; hero in the war between the Greeks and the Trojans

Aeneas Trojan hero who founded Rome; son of Aphrodite (Venus) and the Trojan Anchises

Aeneid epic by the Roman poet Virgil about the legendary hero Aeneas and the founding of Rome

Agamemnon Greek king and commander of Greek forces in the Trojan War; later killed by his wife, Clytemnestra

Ajax Greek hero of the Trojan War

Amazons female warriors in Greek mythology

Aphrodite Greek goddess of love and beauty (identified with the Roman goddess Venus)

Apollo Greek god of the sun, the arts, medicine, and herdsmen; son of Zeus and Leto and twin brother of Artemis

Ares Greek god of war; son of Zeus and Hera (identified with the Roman god Mars)

Artemis in Greek mythology, virgin goddess of the hunt; daughter of Zeus and Leto and twin sister of Apollo (identified with the Roman goddess Diana)

Arthurian legends stories about the life and court of King Arthur of Britain

Asia Minor ancient term for modern-day Turkey, the part of Asia closest to Greece

Assyria kingdom of the ancient Near East located between the Tigris and Euphrates Rivers

Athena in Greek mythology, goddess of wisdom and war; the daughter of Zeus (Roman goddess Minerva)

Atlas Titan in Greek mythology who held the world on his shoulders

Baal god of the ancient Near East associated with fertility and rain

Babylonia ancient kingdom of Mesopotamia; **Babylon** city in Babylonia; **Babylonians** (noun) people of Babylonia; **Babylonian** (adj) referring to kingdom or people

Brahma Hindu creator god

Canaan name given to Palestine and Syria in ancient times; **Canaanites** people of Canaan

Celtic referring to the **Celts,** early inhabitants of Britain whose culture survived in Ireland, Scotland, Wales, Cornwall, and Brittany

Ceres Roman goddess of vegetation and fertility; mother of Proserpina (Greek goddess Demeter)

Cronus Greek deity, king of the Titans; son of Uranus and Gaia

Cyclopes one-eyed giants in Greek mythology

Delphi town on the slopes of Mount Parnassus in Greece that was the site of Apollo's temple and the Delphic oracle

Demeter Greek goddess of vegetation; sister of Zeus and mother of Persephone (Roman goddess Ceres)

Devi Hindu goddess; wife of the god Shiva

Diana Roman goddess of hunting and childbirth (Greek goddess Artemis)

Dionysus Greek god of wine and fertility; son of Zeus by Theban princess Semele (Roman god Bacchus)

Druids priests and political leaders of an ancient Celtic religious order

Euripides (ca. 480–406 B.C.) Greek playwright who wrote many tragedies

Franks early Germanic people who invaded and eventually ruled Gaul (present-day France) between the A.D. 200s and the mid-800s

Golden Fleece hide of a magic ram that hung in a sacred grove guarded by a serpent

Hades Greek god of the underworld; brother of Zeus and husband of Persephone (Roman god Pluto)

Hector in Greek mythology, a Trojan prince and hero in the Trojan War

Helen of Troy in Greek mythology, a beautiful woman and the wife of the king of Sparta; her kidnapping by a Trojan prince led to the Trojan War

Hephaestus Greek god of fire and crafts; son of Zeus and Hera and husband of Aphrodite (Roman god Vulcan)

Hera Greek goddess, wife and sister of Zeus; queen of heaven (Roman goddess Juno)

Hercules (Heracles) Greek hero who had 12 labors to perform; Roman god of strength

Hermes in Greek mythology, the messenger of the gods; escorted the dead to the underworld (Roman god Mercury)

Hesiod (ca. 700 B.C.) Greek poet who wrote the *Theogony*

Homer (ca. 700s B.C.) Greek poet thought to be the author of the great epics the *Iliad* and the *Odyssey*

Iliad Greek epic poem about the Trojan War composed by Homer

Indo-Iranian having to do with the peoples and cultures of northern India, Pakistan, Afghanistan, and Iran

Isis Egyptian goddess of rebirth and resurrection; mother of Horus

Jason Greek hero and leader of the Argonauts who went on a quest for the Golden Fleece

Jupiter Roman god of the sky and ruler of the other gods (Greek god Zeus)

Mars Roman god of war (Greek god Ares)

Medusa in Greek mythology, a monster whose hair was made of snakes and whose face turned humans to stone

Mercury Roman messenger god (Greek god Hermes)

Mesopotamia area between the Tigris and Euphrates Rivers, most of present-day Iraq

Metamorphoses narrative poem by the Roman author Ovid

Mongol referring to an empire in southeastern Asia that existed from about 1200 to the 1700s

Neptune in Roman mythology, god of the sea (the Greeks called him Poseidon)

Norse referring to the people and culture of Scandinavia: Norway, Sweden, Denmark, and Iceland

Odin in Norse mythology, one-eyed deity and ruler of the gods

Odysseus Greek hero who journeyed for ten years to return home after the Trojan War

Odyssey epic by the Greek poet Homer that tells the story of the journey of the hero Odysseus

Oedipus in Greek mythology, king of Thebes

Olympus in Greek mythology, home of the gods

Orpheus Greek hero known for his musical skills; son of Apollo and Calliope

Osiris in Egyptian mythology, the chief god of death

Ovid (ca. 43 B.C.–A.D. 17) Roman poet who wrote the *Metamorphoses*

Palestine ancient land located on the site of modern Israel and part of Jordan

Pegasus in Greek mythology, a winged horse

Perseus Greek hero, son of Danaë and Zeus, who cut off the head of Medusa

Persia ancient land in southwestern Asia, including much of present-day Iran and Afghanistan

Philistines ancient people who lived along the coast of Canaan (present-day Palestine and Syria)

Phoenicia ancient maritime country located in an area that is now part of Lebanon

Phrygia ancient country located in present-day Turkey

Pindar (ca. 522–438 B.C.) Greek poet

Plutarch (ca. A.D. 46–120) Greek author who wrote biographies of important Greeks and Romans

Poseidon Greek god, ruler of the sea, and brother of Zeus (Roman god Neptune)

Prometheus in Greek mythology, Titan said to have created the human race

Pueblos Native American groups of the southwestern United States, including the Hopi, Keresan, Tewa, Tiwa, and Zuni

Quetzalcoatl Feathered Serpent god of Central America; Aztec god of learning and creation

Ra (Re) in Egyptian mythology, the sun god

Saturn Roman god of the harvest

Semitic relating to people of the ancient Near East, including Jews, Arabs, Babylonians, Assyrians, and Phoenicians

Set in Egyptian mythology, god of the sun and sky; brother of Osiris

Sophocles (ca. 496–406 B.C.) Greek playwright who wrote many tragedies

Sparta ancient Greek city-state

Sumer part of ancient Babylonia in southern Mesopotamia; **Sumerians** people of Sumer

Thebes ancient Egyptian city on the Nile River

Theogony epic written by the Greek poet Hesiod explaining the creation of the world and the birth of the gods

Theseus Greek hero who killed the Minotaur of Crete with Ariadne, the daughter of King Minos of Crete

Thor in Norse mythology, the thunder god

Titan one of a family of giants who ruled the earth until overthrown by the Greek gods of Olympus

Trojan War legendary war between the Greeks and the people of Troy that was set off by the kidnapping of Helen, wife of the king of Sparta; inspiration for Homer's epics the *Iliad* and the *Odyssey*

Troy ancient city that was the site of the Trojan War; present-day Turkey near the Dardanelles

Valhalla in Norse mythology, the home of the dead heroes

Valkyrie in Norse mythology, one of the handmaidens to the god Odin

Virgil (ca. 70–19 B.C.) Roman poet who wrote the *Aeneid* explaining the founding of Rome

Vishnu Hindu god, preserver and restorer

Vulcan Roman god of fire (Greek god Hephaestus)

Zeus in Greek mythology, king of the gods and husband of Hera (Roman god Jupiter)

Family Trees *and Leading Figures in World Mythology*

Family trees of gods and other figures in Greek, Norse, Arthurian, Egyptian, and Babylonian mythology appear on the following pages. Few of the characters of South American, African, Oceanic, Native American, and Asian mythology are members of the same family, but charts of the major figures appear throughout the encyclopedia. A list of these charts is found on page x of volume 1.

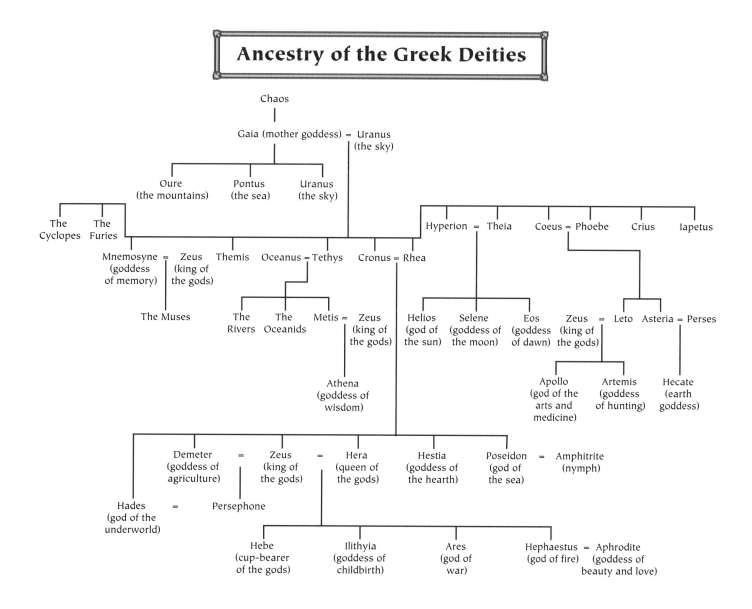

Ancestry of the Greek Deities

Descendants of Leda

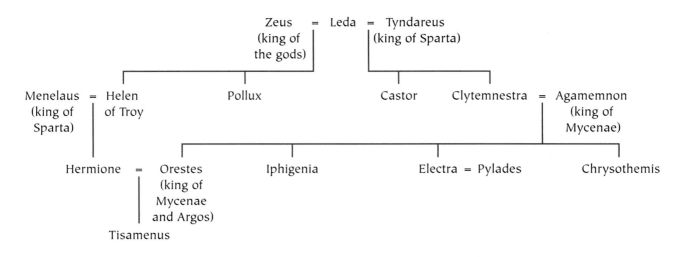

House of Troy

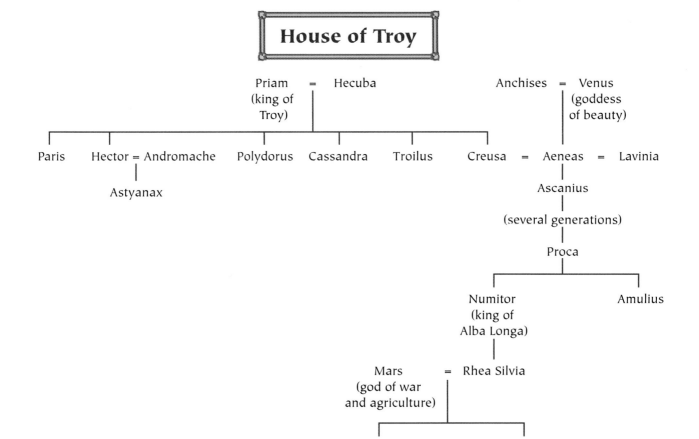

Babylonian Deities

Tiamat = Apsu
(goddess of the | (god of the
salt waters) | sweet waters)

Ansar = Kisar
(primordial male figure | (primordial female figure
representing heaven) | representing earth)

Sin Anu = Antu
(moon god) (chief sky
god)

Shamash Ishtar Ea = Damkina Enlil
(sun god) (goddess (god of (god of wind
of love) water) and land)

Marduk
(chief god)

Nabu
(god of wisdom
and writing)

Egyptian Deities

Amun-Re ········· Amun ········· Ra or Re ········· Atum ········· Ra-Atum
(supreme sun god)

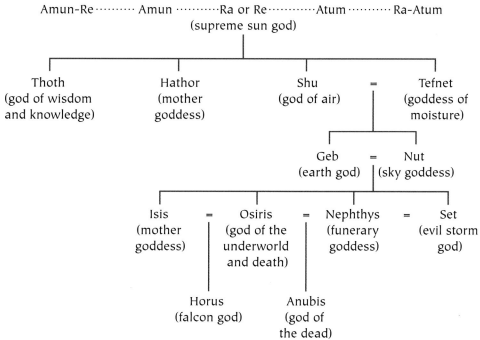

Thoth Hathor Shu = Tefnet
(god of wisdom (mother (god of air) (goddess of
and knowledge) goddess) moisture)

Geb = Nut
(earth god) (sky goddess)

Isis = Osiris = Nephthys = Set
(mother (god of the (funerary (evil storm
goddess) underworld goddess) god)
and death)

Horus Anubis
(falcon god) (god of
the dead)

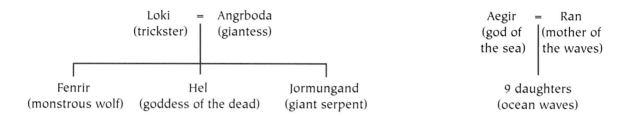

Norse Deities and Other Supernatural Beings

Loki (trickster) = Angrboda (giantess)

Aegir (god of the sea) = Ran (mother of the waves)

Fenrir (monstrous wolf)

Hel (goddess of the dead)

Jormungand (giant serpent)

9 daughters (ocean waves)

Aesir

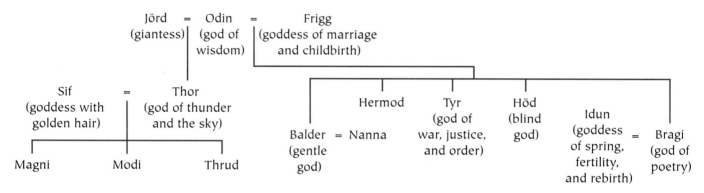

Jörd (giantess) = Odin (god of wisdom) = Frigg (goddess of marriage and childbirth)

Sif (goddess with golden hair) = Thor (god of thunder and the sky)

Magni

Modi

Thrud

Hermod

Tyr (god of war, justice, and order)

Höd (blind god)

Idun (goddess of spring, fertility, and rebirth) = Bragi (god of poetry)

Balder (gentle god) = Nanna

Vanir

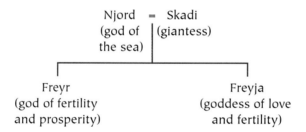

Njord (god of the sea) = Skadi (giantess)

Freyr (god of fertility and prosperity)

Freyja (goddess of love and fertility)

Major Figures in Arthurian Legends

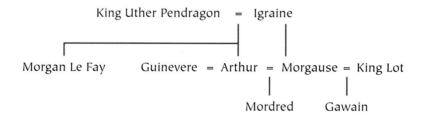

King Uther Pendragon = Igraine

Morgan Le Fay

Guinevere = Arthur = Morgause = King Lot

Mordred

Gawain

Arthur's Court

Lancelot, knight of the Round Table
Galahad, knight of the Round Table
Merlin, wizard

Suggested Readings

World Mythology and General Reference

Andrews, Tamra. *Legends of the Earth, Sea, and Sky.* New York: Oxford University Press, 2000.

Bierlein, J. F. *Parallel Myths.* New York: Ballantine Books, 1994.

Campbell, Joseph. *The Hero with a Thousand Faces.* New York: MJF Books, 1996.

_____. *The Masks of God.* 4 vols. New York: Arkana, 1991.

Cooper, J. C., ed. *Brewer's Book of Myth and Legend.* New York: Cassell, 1992.

*Cotterell, Arthur. *The Macmillan Illustrated Encyclopedia of Myths and Legends.* New York: Macmillan Publishing Company, 1989.

*_____. *The Dictionary of Mythology.* Oxford: Oxford University Press, 1992.

Coulter, Charles R., and Patricia Turner. *Encyclopedia of Ancient Deities.* Jefferson, N.C.: McFarland, 2000.

Eliot, Alexander. *The Universal Myths: Heroes, Gods, Tricksters, and Others.* New York: Truman Talley Books/Meridian, 1976.

Frazer, Sir James, and Theodor H. Gaster. *The New Golden Bough.* New York: The New American Library, 1959.

*Hallam, Elizabeth. *Gods and Goddesses: A Treasury of Deities and Tales from World Mythology.* New York: Macmillan, 1996.

Jordan, Michael. *Myths of the World: A Thematic Encyclopedia.* London: Kyle Cathie LTD, 1993.

Leeming, David Adams. *The World of Myth.* New York: Oxford University Press, 1990.

Lindahl, Carl, John McNamara, and John Lindow, eds. *Medieval Folklore: An Encyclopedia of Myths, Legends, Tales, Beliefs, and Customs.* 2 vols. Santa Barbara, Calif.: ABC-CLIO, 2000.

McLeish, Kenneth. *Myths and Legends of the World Explored.* London: Bloomsbury, 1996.

Puhvel, Jaan. *Comparative Mythology.* Baltimore: Johns Hopkins University Press, 1987.

Rosenberg, Donna. *Folklore, Myths, and Legends: A World Perspective.* Lincolnwood, Ill.: NTC Publishing Group, 1997.

_____. *World Mythology.* Lincolnwood, Ill.: NTC Publishing Group, 1994.

Sykes, Egerton. *Who's Who in Non-Classical Mythology.* New York: Oxford University Press, 1993.

*Wilkinson, Philip. *Illustrated Dictionary of Mythology: Heroes, Heroines, Gods, and Goddesses from Around the World.* London: Dorling Kindersley Limited, 1998.

*Willis, Roy, ed. *World Mythology.* New York: Henry Holt and Company, 1993.

North America

Bierhorst, John. *The Mythology of North America.* New York: William Morrow and Company, Inc., 1985.

Burland, Cottie. *North American Indian Mythology.* New York: Peter Bedrick Books, 1987.

Clark, Ella E. *Indian Legends of the Pacific Northwest.* Los Angeles: University of California Press, 1953.

Dauenhauer, Nora Marks, and Richard Dauenhauer, ed. *Haa shuká, Our Ancestors: Tlingit Oral Narratives.* Seattle: University of Washington Press; Juneau: Sealaska Heritage Foundation, 1987.

Davis, Mary B. *Native America in the Twentieth Century.* New York: Garland Publishing, Inc., 1996.

Erdoes, Richard, and Alfonso Ortiz, eds. *American Indian Myths and Legends.* New York: Pantheon Books, 1984.

Gill, Sam D., and Irene F. Sullivan. *Dictionary of Native American Mythology.* New York: Oxford University Press, 1992.

Leeming, David, and Jake Page. *Myths, Legends, and Folktales of America, An Anthology.* New York: Oxford University Press, 1999.

_____. *The Mythology of Native North America.* Norman, Okla.: University of Oklahoma Press, 1998.

Newcomb, Franc Johnson. *Navaho Folk Tales.* Albuquerque: University of New Mexico Press, 1991.

Penn, W. S., ed. *The Telling of the World, Native American Stories and Art.* New York: Stewart, Tabori, and Chang, 1996.

Time-Life Books. *The Spirit World.* Alexandria, Va.: Time-Life Books, 1992.

Tlingit Myths and Texts. Recorded by John R. Swanton. St. Clair Shores, Mich.: Scholarly Press, 1976.

Tyler, Hamilton A. *Pueblo Gods and Myths.* Norman, Okla.: University of Oklahoma Press, 1964.

*Asterisk denotes book for young readers.

Wiget, Andrew, ed. *Handbook of Native American Literature*. New York: Garland Publishing, Inc., 1996.

Williamson, Ray A., and Claire R. Farrer, eds. *Earth & Sky*. Albuquerque: University of New Mexico Press, 1992.

Zolbrod, Paul G. *Diné Bahane': The Navajo Creation Story*. Albuquerque: University of New Mexico Press, 1984.

Europe

Ashe, Geoffrey. *Mythology of the British Isles*. North Pomfret, Vt.: Trafalgar Square Publishing, 1990.

Barber, Richard. *Myths and Legends of the British Isles*. Rochester, N.Y.: Boydell Press, 1999.

Coghlan, Ronan. *The Illustrated Encyclopedia of Arthurian Legends*. New York: Barnes and Noble Books, 1995.

*Crossley-Holland, Kevin. *The Norse Myths*. New York: Pantheon Books, 1980.

Davidson, Ellis H. R. *Gods and Myths of Northern Europe*. New York: Penguin Books, 1990.

____. *Scandinavian Mythology*. New York: Peter Bedrick Books, 1986.

Delaney, John J. *Pocket Dictionary of Saints*. New York: Image Books Doubleday, 1983.

Ellis, Peter. *Dictionary of Celtic Mythology*. New York: Oxford Press, 1994.

Ferguson, George. *Signs and Symbols in Christian Art*. New York: Oxford University Press, 1961.

Gordon, Anne. *A Book of Saints*. New York: Bantam Books, 1994.

Green, Miranda J. *Dictionary of Celtic Myth and Legend*. New York: Thames and Hudson, 1992.

Hatto, A. T., trans. *Nibelungenlied: A New Translation*. New York: Penguin Books, 1969.

Heaney, Seamus, trans. *Beowulf*. New York: Farrar Straus & Giroux, 2000.

Lönnrot, Elias. *The Kalevala*. Translated by Francis Peabody Magoun, Jr. Cambridge, Mass.: Harvard University Press, 1963.

MacCana, Proinsias. *Celtic Mythology*. London: The Hamlyn Publishing Group Limited, 1970.

Orchard, Andy. *Dictionary of Norse Myth and Legend*. London: Cassell, 1997.

Ancient Greece and Rome

Bulfinch, Thomas. *Bulfinch's Mythology*. New York: Modern Library, 1998.

*Colcum, Padraic. *The Children's Homer: The Adventures of Odysseus and the Tale of Troy*. New York: Aladdin Paperbacks, 1946.

*Daly, Kathleen. *Greek and Roman Mythology A to Z: A Young Reader's Companion*. New York: Facts on File, 1992.

*D'Aulaire, Ingri, and Edgar Parin D'Aulaire. *Book of Greek Myths*. New York: Bantam Doubleday Dell Publishing Group, Inc., 1962.

Dixon-Kennedy, Mike. *Encyclopedia of Greco-Roman Mythology*. Santa Barbara, Calif.: ABC-CLIO, 1998.

*Green, Roger Lancelyn. *Tales of the Greek Heroes*. London: Penguin Books, 1994.

Hamilton, Edith. *Mythology*. Boston: Little, Brown and Company, 1946.

Harvey, Paul. *The Oxford Companion to Classical Literature*. New York: Oxford University Press, 1984.

Hazel, John, and Michael Grant. *Who's Who in Classical Mythology*. New York: Oxford University Press, 1993.

Homer. *Iliad*. Translated by Robert Fagles. New York: Viking, 1990.

Homer. *Odyssey*. Translated by Robert Fagles. New York: Viking, 1996.

Hornblower, Simon, and Antony Spawforth, eds. *The Oxford Classical Dictionary*. Oxford: Oxford University Press, 1996.

*Lies, Betty Bonham. *Earth's Daughters: Stories of Women in Classical Mythology*. Golden, Colo.: Fulcrum Resources, 1999.

*McCaughrean, Geraldine. *Greek Myths*. New York: Maxwell Macmillan International, 1993.

*Osborne, Mary Pope. *Favorite Greek Myths*. New York: Scholastic, Inc., 1989.

Ovid. *Metamorphoses*. Translated by Rolfe Humphries. Bloomington: Indiana University Press, 1955.

Radice, Betty. *Who's Who in the Ancient World*. New York: Penguin Books, 1973.

*Russell, William F. *Classic Myths to Read Aloud*. New York: Three Rivers Press, 1989.

*Switzer, Ellen Eichenwald. *Greek Myths: Gods, Heroes, and Monsters: Their Sources, Their Stories, and Their Meanings*. New York: Atheneum, 1988.

Africa

Arnott, Kathleen. *African Myths and Legends*. New York: Oxford University Press, 1996.

Courlander, Harold. *A Treasury of African Folklore*. New York: Crown Publishers, Inc., 1975.

Ford, Clyde W. *The Hero with an African Face: Mythic Wisdom of Traditional Africa*. New York: Bantam Books, 1999.

Knappert, Jan. *Kings, Gods, and Spirits from African Mythology.* New York: Peter Bedrick Books, 1995.

Parrinder, Geoffrey. *African Mythology.* New York: Peter Bedrick Books, 1982.

Radin, Paul A., ed. *African Folktales.* New York: Schocken Books, 1983.

Scheub, Harold. *Dictionary of African Mythology: The Mythmaker as Storyteller.* New York: Oxford University Press, 2000.

Egypt and the Near East

Andrews, Carol, ed. *The Ancient Egyptian Book of the Dead.* Translated by R. O. Faulkner. New York: Macmillan, 1985.

Black, Jeremy, and Anthony Green. *Gods, Demons, and Symbols of Ancient Mesopotamia.* Austin: University of Texas Press, 1997.

Bratton, Fred Gladstone. *Myths and Legends of the Ancient Near East.* New York: Barnes & Noble, 1993.

Burton, Sir Richard F. *The Arabian Nights.* New York: Blue Ribbon Books, Inc., 1932.

Graves, Robert, and Raphael Patai. *Hebrew Myths: The Book of Genesis.* New York: Greenwich House, 1983.

*Gray, John. *Near Eastern Mythology.* New York: Peter Bedrick Books, 1982.

Hart, George. *A Dictionary of Egyptian Gods and Goddesses.* New York: Routledge, 1993.

Hooke, S. H. *Middle Eastern Mythology.* New York: Penguin Books, 1991.

Jackson, Danny P. *The Epic of Gilgamesh.* Wauconda, Ill.: Blochazy-Carducci Publishers, 1997.

King, L. W., ed. *Enuma Elish: The Seven Tablets of Creation.* New York: AMS Press, 1976.

Leick, Gwendolyn. *A Dictionary of Ancient Near Eastern Mythology.* New York: Routledge, 1998.

McCall, Henrietta. *Mesopotamian Myths.* Austin: University of Texas Press, 1993.

Quirke, Stephen. *Ancient Egyptian Religion.* New York: Dover Publications, 1997.

Oceania: Australia, Melanesia, Micronesia, and Polynesia

Andersen, Johannes C. *Myths and Legends of the Polynesians.* New York: Dover Publications, Inc., 1995.

Berndt, Ronald, and Catherine Berndt. *The World of the First Australians: Aboriginal Traditional Life Past and Present.* Canberra, Australia: Aboriginal Studies Press, 1996.

Craig, Robert D. *Dictionary of Polynesian Mythology.* New York: Greenwood Press, 1989.

Leenhardt, Maurice. *Do Kamo: Person and Myth in the Melanesian World.* Chicago: University of Chicago Press, 1979.

*Poigant, Roslyn. *Oceanic Mythology.* New York: The Hamlyn Publishing Group, 1967.

Reed, A. W. *Aboriginal Myths, Legends, and Fables.* Chatswood, Australia: William Heinemann Australia, 1993.

*Roberts, Melva Jean. *Dreamtime Heritage: Australian Aboriginal Myths.* Adelaide, Australia: Rigby Limited, 1979.

Spriggs, Matthew. *The Island Melanesians.* Oxford, UK; Cambridge, Mass.: Blackwell, 1997.

Sutton, Peter. *Dreamings: The Art of Aboriginal Australia.* New York: George Braziller, 1988.

Asia

Buck, William, trans. *Mahabharata.* Berkeley, Calif.: University of California Press, 1981.

_____. *Ramayana.* Berkeley, Calif.: University of California Press, 1981.

*Christie, Anthony. *Chinese Mythology.* New York: Peter Bedrick Books, 1983.

Coomaraswamy, Amanda, and Sister Nivedita. *Myths of the Hindus and Buddhists.* New York: Dover Publications, Inc., 1967.

Davis, F. Hadland. *Myths and Legends of Japan.* New York: Dover Publications, 1992.

Dimmitt, Cornelia, and J. A. B. van Buitenen, ed., trans. *Classical Hindu Mythology: A Reader in the Sanskrit Puranas.* Philadelphia: Temple University Press, 1978.

*Ions, Veronica. *Indian Mythology.* New York: Peter Bedrick Books, 1983.

Jayakar, Pupul. *The Earth Mother: Legends, Ritual Arts, and Goddesses of India.* San Francisco: Harper & Row Publishers, 1990.

McAlpine, Helen, and William McAlpine. *Japanese Tales and Legends.* New York: Oxford University Press, 1996.

O'Flaherty, Wendy Doniger, trans. *Rig Veda.* New York: Penguin Books, 1981.

*Piggot, Juliet. *Japanese Mythology.* New York: Peter Bedrick Books, 1982.

Prabhavananda, Swami, and Christopher Isherwood, trans. *The Song of God: Bhagavad Gita.* New York: NAL, 1993.

*Sanders, Tao Tao Liu. *Dragons, Gods & Spirits from Chinese Mythology.* New York: Peter Bedrick Books, 1995.

Suggested Readings

Tyler, Royall, ed. *Japanese Tales.* New York: Pantheon Books, 1987.

Werner, E. T. C. *Myths and Legends of China.* New York: Dover Publications, Inc., 1994.

Latin America

Bierhorst, John. *The Mythology of Mexico and Central America.* New York: William Morrow and Company, Inc., 1990.

Coe, Michael D. *The Maya.* New York: Thames and Hudson, 1987.

Davies, Nigel. *The Aztecs.* Norman, Okla.: University of Oklahoma Press, 1982.

Miller, Mary, and Karl Taube. *The Gods and Symbols of Ancient Mexico and the Maya.* New York: Thames and Hudson, 1993.

*Nicholson, Irene. *Mexican and Central American Mythology.* New York: Peter Bedrick Books, 1983.

*Osborne, Harold. *South American Mythology.* New York: Peter Bedrick Books, 1983.

Schele, Linda. *A Forest of Kings.* New York: William Morrow and Company, Inc., 1990.

Schele, Linda, and Mary Ellen Miller. *The Blood of Kings.* New York: George Braziller, 1986.

Tedlock, Dennis, trans. *Popol Vuh.* New York: Simon & Schuster, Inc., 1985.

Wolf, Eric. *Sons of the Shaking Earth.* Chicago: University of Chicago Press, 1959.

Online Resources

University of Michigan. *Provides information about figures and stories from world mythology.*
http://www.windows.umich.edu/cgi-bin/tour.cgi?link=/mythology/mythology.html

World Mythology. *Provides links to numerous sites containing information about myths and legends of the world.*
http://pubpages.unh.edu/~cbsiren/myth2.html

University of Pittsburgh. *Sites contains information about characters and stories from myths and legends.*
http://www.pitt.edu/~dash/mythlinks.html
http://www.pitt.edu/~dash/folktexts.html

Encyclopedia Mythica. *Provides information about the myths and legends of many places in the world.*
http://www.pantheon.org/mythica

Bulfinch's Mythology. *Online version of author's book on mythology with stories about classical gods and goddesses and Arthurian legends.*
http://www.bulfinch.org

University of Evansville. *Provides links to online resources for ancient and medieval history.*
http://argos.evansville.edu

Mythical Quests and Journeys. *Provides information about many of the trips and travels of mythological figures.*
http://portico.bl.uk/exhibitions/mythical

Temple University. *Contains useful information from Classical Mythology, including glossaries of names and phrases, genealogical charts, and maps of voyages.*
http://www.temple.edu/classics/mythdirectory.html

Tufts University Perseus Website. *Contains information and stories from Greek and Roman Mythology.*
http://www.perseus.tufts.edu

Text of the *Iliad* and the *Odyssey. Provides online translations of these two epic poems by Homer.*
http://www.uoregon.edu/~joelja/iliad.html
http://www.uoregon.edu/~joelja/odyssey.html

Hinduism and Mythology. *Provides information about Hindu deities, myths, and legends.*
http://members.tripod.com/~srinivasp/mythology/index.html
http://www.hindumythology.com/index.html

Norse Mythology. *Contains descriptions of Norse gods and goddesses and major stories from Norse mythology.*
http://www.ugcs.caltech.edu/~cherryne/mythology.html

Egyptian Mythology. *Gives descriptions about gods, goddesses, and religion of the ancient Egyptians.*
http://www.EgyptianMyths.com/index.html

Maya Civilization. *Provides information on Mayan history, culture, and religion.*
http://civilization.ca/membrs/civiliz/maya/mmc01eng.html

Aztec History. *Contains information about Aztec religion, culture, and history.*
http://northcoast.com/~spdtom/aztec.html

Photo Credits

Volume 1

Archivo Iconografico, S.A./Corbis: 133
Corbis/Paul Almasy: 27
Corbis/Archivo Iconografico, S.A.: 9, 33, 90
Corbis/Arte & Immagini srl: 2
Corbis/Asian Art & Archaeology, Inc.: 32
Corbis/Bettmann: 19, 39
Corbis/Bojan Brecelj: 35
Corbis/Dean Conger: 108
Corbis/Richard A. Cooke: 83
Corbis/Leonard de Selva: 5
Corbis/Mimmo Jodice: 70, 118
Corbis/Massimo Listri: 120
Corbis/Francis G. Mayer: 52
Corbis/Gianni Dagli Orti: 80, 102
Corbis/Sakamoto Photo Research Laboratory: 110
Corbis/Penny Tweedie: 77
Giraudon/Art Resource, New York: 129

The Granger Collection, New York: 14, 22, 64, 88, 93, 104, 112, 115, 134
Holton Collection/SuperStock: 43
Erich Lessing/Art Resource, New York: 68, 74, 116, 123
Nimatallah/Art Resource, New York: 29
Gianni Dagli Orti/Corbis: 61
Private Collection/Bridgeman Art Library: 138
Neil Rabinowitz/Corbis: 45
Royal Library, Copenhagen, Denmark/Bridgeman Art Library: 87
Scala/Art Resource, New York: 12
Seattle Art Museum, Gift of John H. Hauberg: 96
Vanni Archive/Corbis: 126
Victoria and Albert Museum, London/Art Resource, New York: 99

Volume 2

Archivo Iconografico, S. A./Corbis: 16, 31
Arte & Immagini srl/Corbis: 92
Bettmann/Corbis: 23, 81, 83, 147
Jonathan Blair/Corbis: 11
Burstein Collection/Corbis: 134
Fitzwilliam Museum, University of Cambridge/Bridgeman Art Library: 126
Fogg Art Museum, Harvard University, Gift of Meta and Paul J. Sachs/Bridgeman Art Library: 76
Werner Forman/Art Resource, New York: 7, 8, 106, 148
Gallen-Kalle'la/AKG London: 59
Giraudon/Art Resource, New York: 87
The Granger Collection, New York: 37, 55, 104, 124, 131, 138, 142
Hermitage Museum, St. Petersburg/Leonid Bogdanov/SuperStock: 109
Mimmo Jodice/Corbis: 71
Erich Lessing/Art Resource, New York: 96, 103
Maas Gallery, London/Bridgeman Art Library: 39
Metropolitan Museum of Art, New York/Bridgeman Art Library: 49
National Library of Australia, Canberra/Bridgeman Art Library: 62

National Museum of American Art, Washington DC/Art Resource, New York: 2
Michael Nicholson/Corbis: 21
Nimatallah/Art Resource, New York: 99
Gianni Dagli Orti/Corbis: 120, 135, 137
Private Collection/Bridgeman Art Library: 26
Carmen Redondo/Corbis: 42
Royal Albert Memorial Museum, Exeter, Devon, UK/Bridgeman Art Library: 53
Rumtek Tibetan Monastery, India/Chigmaroff/Davison/SuperStock: 70
Scala/Art Resource, New York: 144, 150
Kurt Scholz/SuperStock: 46
Seattle Art Museum, Gift of John H. Hauberg: 84
Sistine Chapel, Rome/SuperStock: 113
Keren Su/Corbis: 34
SuperStock: 128
Tate Gallery, London/Art Resource, New York: 90
Gian Berto Vanni/Corbis: 12
Victoria and Albert Museum, London/Bridgeman Art Library: 66
Victoria and Albert Museum, London/Art Resource, New York: 132

Photo Credits

Cultures Index

Africa

Aiwel, **1**:28
Ala, **1**:30
Amma, **1**:34
Anansi, **1**:36
Brer Rabbit, **1**:105
Cagn, **1**:114
Eshu, **2**:52–55
genies, **2**:82

Ile-Ife, **2**:141–42
Katonda, **3**:19
Kibuka, **3**:19
Lebe, **3**:26
Leza, **3**:27
Mujaji, **3**:71
Mulungu, **3**:71
Mwindo, **3**:72–73

mythology of, **1**:13–18
Nummo, **3**:95–96
Nyame, **3**:97
Ogun, **3**:108
Olorun, **3**:109–10
Sheba, Queen of, **4**:40
Sunjata, **4**:53–54

Ancient Greece and Rome

Acastus, **1**:1
Achilles, **1**:1–3
Adonis, **1**:5–6
Aeneas, **1**:6–9
Aeneid, **1**:10–13
Aeolus, **1**:13
Agamemnon, **1**:24–26
Ajax, **1**:28–29
Amazons, **1**:32–33
ambrosia, **1**:33–34
Amphitryon, **1**:34–35
Androcles, **1**:37
Andromache, **1**:37
Andromeda, **1**:38
Antaeus, **1**:46–47
Apollo, **1**:51–53
Arachne, **1**:53
Arcadia, **1**:53–54
Ares, **1**:54
Argonauts, **1**:54–57
Argus, **1**:58
Ariadne, **1**:58
Asclepius, **1**:66
Astyanax, **1**:67
Atalanta, **1**:67–68
Athena, **1**:69–72
Atlantis, **1**:72–73
Atlas, **1**:73–74
Attis, **1**:74–75
Aurora, **1**:75
Bacchus. *See* Dionysus
Baucis and Philemon, **1**:89
Bellerophon, **1**:89–90
Boreas, **1**:103
Cadmus, **1**:113

caduceus, **1**:113–14
Calliope, **1**:115
Callisto, **1**:115
Calypso, **1**:115–16
Cassandra, **1**:118–19
Cassiopea, **1**:119
Castor and Pollux, **1**:119–21
centaurs, **1**:125–27
Cephalus and Procris, **1**:27
Cerberus, **1**:127
Ceres. *See* Demeter
Circe, **1**:138–40
Clytemnestra, **1**:140
Coriolanus, **1**:141
Cronus, **2**:10
Cupid. *See* Eros
Cybele, **2**:14
Cyclopes, **2**:15
Daedalus, **2**:15–16
Damocles, sword of, **2**:17
Danaë, **2**:18
Daphnis and Chloe, **2**:18–19
Delphi, **2**:19–21
Demeter, **2**:21–22
Diana, **2**:28–29
Dido, **2**:29
Dionysus, **2**:30–32
Electra, **2**:49
Elysium, **2**:50
Eros, **2**:52
Eurydice, **2**:53–54
Fates, **2**:54–56
Furies, **2**:78–79
Gaia, **2**:79
Galatea, **2**:80

Ganymede, **2**:82
giants, **2**:84–85
Golden Bough, **2**:89–90
Golden Fleece, **2**:90–91
Gordian Knot, **2**:92
Gorgons, **2**:92
Graces, **2**:93
Greek mythology, **2**:93–101
Hades, **2**:102–3
Halcyone, **2**:103–4
Harpies, **2**:105
Hecate, **2**:107–8
Hector, **2**:108–9
Hecuba, **2**:109–10
Helen of Troy, **2**:111–13
Hephaestus. *See* Vulcan
Hera, **2**:116–18
Hercules, **2**:118–21
Hermaphroditus, **2**:121
Hermes, **2**:121–22
Hero and Leander, **2**:122
Homer, **2**:135
Horatii, **2**:136
Horatius, **2**:136
Hydra, **2**:140
Hypnos, **2**:140
Iliad, **2**:143–45
Io, **2**:151
Iphigenia, **3**:1
Janus, **3**:6
Jason, **3**:11–13
Jocasta, **3**:15
Juno. *See* Hera
Jupiter. *See* Zeus
Laocoön, **3**:24

Asia

Egypt and Near East

Europe

Cumulative Index

Italicized page numbers refer to illustrations or charts.

Index

Index

Index

Index

Index